CONTINUOUS CONTAINER GARDENS

CONTINUOUS CONTAINER GARDENS

Swap In the Plants of the Season to Create Fresh Designs Year-Round

Sara Begg Townsend
&
Roanne Robbins

Photography by John Gruen

Storey Publishing

The mission of Storey Publishing is to serve our customers by
publishing practical information that encourages
personal independence in harmony with the environment.

Edited by Carleen Madigan
Art direction and book design by Mary Winkelman Velgos
Text production by Jennifer Jepson Smith
Photography by © John Gruen
Indexed by Christine R. Lindemer, Boston Road Communications

Storey Publishing
210 MASS MoCA Way
North Adams, MA 01247
www.storey.com

Printed in China by R.R. Donnelley
10 9 8 7 6 5 4 3 2 1

LIBRARY OF CONGRESS CATALOGING-IN-PUBLICATION DATA

Townsend, Sara Begg.
  Continuous container gardens / by Sara Begg Townsend and Roanne Robbins.
    p. cm.
  Includes index.
  ISBN 978-1-60342-702-9 (pbk. : alk. paper)
  1. Container gardening. I. Robbins, Roanne. II. Title.
SB418.T69 2011
635.9'86—dc22
                                    2010030123

To Dave — SBT

To Ken, Nora, and my family — RR

ACKNOWLEDGMENTS

There are many people to thank in a project such as this. First, thank you to all of the garden owners who were so kind and generous — letting us traipse through their gardens each season in pursuit of the perfect photo. They are Celeste and Jack Penney; Liz Coxe; Virginia and David Merriman; Nancy Hemenway and Ellen Langer; Janet Hadley; Gary and Sue Hanson; Maida, Adam, Prosper, Oscar, and Violet van Dale; and the Little Compton Historical Society. We are grateful to a number of plantspeople for their support of this book: Wayne Mezzitt and Weston Nurseries; Rick Peckham; Leslie and Peter Van Berkum; Tony Elliot; Neil Van Sloun and Sylvan Nursery; Chris Faria and Jim Glover. We're also grateful to Heather Quinlan, Lexy Wright, and Sandy Barrett.

Our thanks to Beth LeComte for all of her awesome help before, during, and after the photo shoots and to Brian and Liz Viera, who saved our backs by letting us use their lift-gate truck. Thank you to our fantastic photographer, John Gruen, who was always a delight to work with and who always came prepared with a stream of movie quotes and entertaining voicemail messages from his son Ben. We thank our editor, Carleen Madigan, whose enthusiasm, patience, and clear mind made the whole thing fun. And finally we thank our families for supporting us during the last year as we ran around buying plants, planting them, photographing them, moving them, and then writing about them. Thank you all!

Contents

PART 1: A NEW TAKE ON CONTAINER GARDENING

PART 2: TWELVE CONTAINERS THROUGH THE YEAR

NOTES FROM SARA'S GARDEN

SOME GARDENING friends once said to me, while I was bemoaning the small size of my new garden, that in many ways a smaller garden is better than a large one. A small garden has the potential to inspire more creativity because it allows the gardener to focus on less and to really perfect it.

This could not be truer for container gardens. The smallness of the container enables me to explore plants and to experiment with new designs. It also allows me to take very good care of my plants; after all, deadheading a container garden takes about 30 seconds, especially if it's done a couple of times a week.

I love the way container gardens bring the garden right up close. I always make sure that at least two of my containers are somewhere along my daily route, whether that's to and from the compost pile or near the path from the house to the sidewalk. After all, how often do you really get down (or up close) and notice the detailed intricacies of a plant — the soft fuzz of a wild ginger (*Asarum canadense*), the strange but magical colors and patterns on a new barrenwort (*Epimedium*) leaf, the breaking bud of a magnolia, or the sweet, unexpected fragrance of a species clematis? It is this level of immersion that we recommend for the maximum enjoyment of the world of plants. It makes your garden a much richer place to be and reminds us of the role each plant plays in the larger garden picture.

Even though Roanne and I both have gardens, we also love trying out new things in containers. I often plant single-specimen containers and mass the pots together. I like being able to protect new, delicate (and sometimes expensive) plants in a container. By planting up single specimens, I get to see if a given plant will do well in a container on its own; if it does, I can include it in a mixed container like the ones we show in this book.

Roanne is truly a master with color; she'll pick a color palette to work with and then push it to the limit in a container. And if she likes it, she'll put it in her own mixed border on a bigger scale, weaving annuals, perennials, and shrubs all together in ways that would never occur to me to try in the border but that look amazing. We should all strive for that boldness — both in a container and in the garden.

Container gardening provides a venue in which you can push the seasons. Walking out your front door on a cool March day and having a container filled with cheery yellow miniature daffodils and grape hyacinths at your feet is like being filled up with a warm, golden ray of happiness. In Cambridge, Massachusetts, where I live, there's no way those bulbs would be up in the garden that early in the year.

Using containers enables us also to push the cultural limits of plants, particularly their soil and light require-ments. For example, our spring underplanting for the birch (*Betula* 'Little King') included a catmint (*Nepeta* 'Little Titch'). Typically, a catmint wouldn't be paired with a woodsy, edge-habitat-loving tree like a birch. The birch loves humus-y, moist soil and can take part shade. The catmint? Not so much. He prefers quick-draining soil and pretty much full sun. But . . . we saw this plant at the nurs-ery and it looked so good, so crisp, just the right colors and textures, that we risked it any-how. We could have left it in the container through the summer to continue providing that great texture and blue-green color, but figured that the plant would have taken much longer to regain its former glory once we planted it out into the garden. It's a trade-off, like many things, so we swapped it out during the next seasonal planting.

Container gardening, espe-cially by the method we're proposing in this book, helps you become a better gardener. The closer you get to your garden and the more success you have, the better gardener you'll become, which will make you want to try a wider range of plants both in your con-tainer and out of it. In container gardening you are forced to learn how to prioritize and how to edit. You learn how to cut something loose if it just isn't working. Limited space lets you focus on the art of combining plants in ways that may not occur to you in a broader-scale garden.

We hope that you will be able to glean some inspiration, beauty, art, and fun from this book and plant them in your containers, your garden, and your world.

Sara Begg Townsend

NOTES FROM ROANNE'S GARDEN

GARDENING IS an art — a creative process — but it is also a living process, governed by time, space, and that mysterious element that one can only describe as *nature*. Your garden can be colorful or neutral, modern or traditional, but no matter what style or look you craft or how much you fuss with the design, nature always has a way of entering your composition, whether you welcome it or not. As the human keepers of these spaces, we decide how much nature we let in. Do we pull the self-sown bronze fennel (*Foeniculum vulgare* 'Bronze'), cut back the enormous butterfly bush (*Buddleia*), terminate weeds with chemicals?

And how do we organize nature? Do we organize by color, by texture, or by sun exposure? Do we arrange plants from tall to short? Bushy to upright? These are just some of the decisions we make to preserve our creation, to feed our desire for control, to design and create something from nothing.

Like a canvas waiting for paint, an empty garden vessel is pure potential. It can be planted to showcase color, to display specimen plants, or to experiment with a subtle composition of textures. It could be planted for function, for practicality, for design, or for pure fun. And because this environment is so much smaller than the garden, we have more control: more control of the conditions, more control of the statement we make, more control of the amount of nature we let in.

We are fortunate to live in a world where unique and enchanting plants are readily available. Whether you find them at a local garden center or order them from specialized growers from afar, you have a whole world of materials at your fingertips, so where do you begin? Maybe the color of bloodtwig dogwood (*Cornus sanguinea*) inspires a start, or it's the endless display of diehard textures in a conifer trough, or perhaps it's the spell of the morning mist lifting off the river and casting a golden glow over the wetland plants. It always works to start with something you love — an inspiration, a color, a texture, a feeling, a statement. What story is this planter trying to convey? What do you aspire to create?

For me, in the examples shown in this book, I am trying to tell a story of nature, of these 12 containers and the environments in which the containers live. By extracting visual elements from the environment, be it an interesting plant attribute like colorful sticks, a seasonal glowing welcome on a winter night, or a fantastic patina on a nearby garden spigot, you can be attentive to the space where you are planting and find the language to tell your story.

Our container story is one that lives in our garden and spans a year in New England. The garden here is ever changing. Leaves come in and out of color, flowers fade and turn to pods or cones, and intricate branches of emptiness blossom with fruit. To garden with trees, shrubs, and perennials is to garden with seasonality — with change. And to us, that is why we use a limited amount of annuals in our combinations.

We moved away from the instant gratification of annuals and opted to create a more garden-inspired mini-landscape. Annual plantings tend to focus on the blossoms — the nonstop dependable color all season long. In our case, flowers are a small part of the equation, a happy bonus that adds depth, surprise, and interest. Blossoms of trees, perennials, and shrubs are just a small part of the plant's life cycle, or, in our perspective, only a small part of the appeal. Our story concerns the artistry of balancing nature's essence as she gently alters texture, color, and feeling with design and the language of the location.

For us, these plants are our environment, and even if they are not the plants that grow in your natural space, we believe that the approach and technique can be customized to any place, season, or time. We hope you will experiment with the ideas and techniques Sara and I share with you, and that you find peace and joy in nature as gardeners, as artists, as storytellers.

Roanne Robbins

INTRODUCTION

The idea for this book evolved as we were working on a story for *Horticulture* magazine. We wanted to show a container as it moved through the seasons, keeping the same vessel but changing out the plants six times a year. Because of the high cost and the large amount of work involved in changing out something so frequently — particularly if you are using beefy, well-grown annuals — we thought perhaps we should scale it back to a seasonal change-out. Then we thought, well, why not focus on one specific attribute in a plant or group of plants, some central quality or characteristic that would help us keep a coherent visual story throughout the seasons? We both love plants and their wild, fantastic diversity, so we thought it would be fun to explore the boundaries of container planting and to incorporate as many perennials, trees, and shrubs as possible, both as large central elements and as the underplantings. This new approach allows us to carry out the more naturalistic planting style that we both prefer, a look that can be more difficult to accomplish when you stick strictly to annuals.

This way of container planting closely mirrors and celebrates the seasonal changes happening in the garden, which allows the containers to be a more visually coherent part of a larger garden space year-round. In some of the containers we demonstrate in this book, we change out almost everything from one season to the next, keeping in only a central plant or two. In others, where the central plants demonstrate a lovely transition through the seasons, we leave in the majority of the planting, with just a plant or two being added to beef up the underplanting. For the winter season, we approach container design almost as if we were designing floral arrangements, filling up gaps in the composition with cut twigs, leaves, boughs, tiny mushrooms, and anything else that catches our eye.

By celebrating the seasons in this way, the gardener has many more opportunities to try out different plant combinations and to extend his or her container gardening season by focusing on the particular glories of each season — be it luscious, creamy-white daffodils in spring or a crisp, corrugated ruby oakleaf hydrangea (*Hydrangea quercifolia*) in autumn. And while the question of cost is always on our minds, it seems to us that although the initial outlay of money may be higher, your long-term cost is lower because your plant purchases are not one-season wonders. Essentially, your container is serving as a beautiful experimental nursery bed for plants you want to get to know before they go in the garden.

Play with Your Plants!

WE HOPE OUR APPROACH to container-garden design will encourage you to:

• Celebrate the diversity of plants and focus on specific qualities, such as unusual bark, cool foliage, delicate seedheads, excellence in shade, and overall beauty through the year (rather than valuing a plant only for its colorful flowers)

• Celebrate unusual plants by bringing their beauty up close

• Focus on seasonality and the new rich-ness that each season brings to the garden

• Use the personal style of your house and garden as a guide for creating exciting container designs

• Approach container-garden design as you would floral design; that is, think about the way a composition is created

• Explore fun, new color palettes and interesting textures on a smaller scale, before committing to their use in the garden

• Create beautiful compositions that can contribute new plant members to your garden party

• Reduce your plant waste by not pur-chasing a lot of "throwaway" annuals.

Part 1

A NEW TAKE ON CONTAINER GARDENING

WHEN MOST PEOPLE think of container gardens, they're likely to envision a home for annual plants — think "pansies in a window box." Annuals are plants that live hard and die young, you might say. They complete their life cycle in one season: they germinate, bloom their hearts out, then become compost. In fact, many beginning gardeners don't think of buying anything *but* annuals when they're planting up a container. Geraniums and impatiens are all well and good in some cases, but you know what? We're ready for a new take on container planting.

Charming ferny *Microbiota decussata* makes an excellent container underplanting.

EXPAND YOUR PLANT WORLD

There are so many reasons to look beyond the usual lineup of annuals for your container. First of all, perennials, shrubs, and trees tend to change with the seasons, and some even have their best moments *after* the frost comes. Many annuals are one-trick ponies — they offer just a single attribute, be it color, leaf texture, or fragrance. If you want just one color or texture all summer, that's great. But it doesn't lend itself to dynamic plantings, since the plants don't change much from month to month.

Another reason to shift away from annuals is that they are throwaway plants. Perennials, shrubs, and trees, which live for more than one season, can either be left in the container until the next spring, or be planted out into the garden. This enables the gardener to play with different combinations on a smaller scale before committing to them in the garden. Annuals stay with you through the growing season and then they go into the

Let your central plant — such as the small, golden-tipped Hinoki cypress at center — drive the design of the composition and the selection of accompanying plants.

compost. Sure, compost is an important part of the garden, but there are certainly less expensive ways to make it! Why spend money (and not an insignificant amount, if you've branched out into some of the more interesting, hard-to-find annuals) on something that's just going to get tossed?

Plant-Driven Style

What we're talking about here is letting your plant selection dictate a stylistic feel for your

container for the entire year. Your favorite shrub, tree, perennial, or grass may not stay in the container throughout the entire growing season, but it can help you create a design plan for the year. If you do pick a shrub or tree to stay in the container through the year, think of it as a backbone for your container — something to provide a structure for the remainder of your planting. For the rest of the year, you can swap the underplantings in and out. Some of them can remain from one season to the next, but many will move out into the garden (or a friend's garden if you don't have one).

While you're at it, why not include other embellishments, like sticks, berried branches, grapevine, mini toadstools, and more? Look in unexpected places, like the floral section of your local grocery store. Play with color, texture, form, and style. Whatever you do, do it confidently.

Really, designing with plants is no different from designing your home living space. Sara explained this to her good friend Blaire, a young mother and a new homeowner with great style and an eye for color and texture. When you walk into her house, you might think a professional designer had helped her. But she's always asking for help with her garden. Sara helps her a bit, but mostly tries to encourage her to take that design confidence outside. It is a different medium, but the same ideas apply. There's really no wrong answer, as long as you think it's beautiful.

We're just here to give you some suggestions, guidelines, and inspiration. Most plants can grow happily in a container for a year or two. So look at everything!

Why Garden in Containers?

A CONTAINER GARDEN is a garden in miniature in a contained and controlled environment. The container can truly be anything and made from anything: terra-cotta, concrete, pressed stone, iron, wood, and many other materials. Many gardeners successfully grow contained gardens in strange yet beautiful found objects (something we don't really advocate, unless you've really got that junk-chic thing down; otherwise it may look like, well, junk). These types of gardens can add luster to a drab corner of the garden where only weeds seem to thrive or accent a special part of your shrub border by drawing the eye.

If the plant or plants you've chosen for your container garden don't love the conditions in the spot you've selected (or if you feel like another place in the garden needs a bit of sparkle), you can always move them. A container's mobility is one of its great benefits; even the heavier ones can be moved with the help of a few strong friends.

Container gardens are important because they enable the gardener to expand her personal plant palette. Even if you've got the most lushly overplanted garden in the ground, a container can be a great way to try something new. They also allow many gardeners to try new plants either in combination with others or on their own. We've just started growing hostas in containers as a way to combat slug madness. We have also been growing bulbs in containers as a way to see them up close and enjoy them in their own shining glory instead of as part of the wilder, woollier landscape. Finally, containers allow gardeners to play without the sometimes overwhelming fear of commitment (although the plants we're suggesting are a bit more of a commitment than a six-pack of lobelia).

Fresh-cut greens, rosy red berries, and sparkly lights add cheer to a winter planting.

PICKING PLANTS

We selected all of our backbone plants based on attributes we love, from beautiful bark, to pretty summer flowers, to great textural leaves, or all of the above. You should do the same. And if you don't know much about plants, take a walk in your neighborhood, go to a local arboretum or botanical garden, ask friends who are plant-lovers. If you feel overwhelmed by options — which happens to the best of us — narrow down the choice by determining where in your garden or outdoor living space your container is going to be sited. Is the location shady, sunny, windy, or protected? Which plants grow well in those conditions?

Evoking a Style

The place where you plan to site your container has bearing not only on the kind of backbone plant you choose but also on the scale of the planting and, most likely, the style of the final composition. For example, when we were choosing our backbone plants, we knew we wanted one

Adding Seasonal Color

Although we're advocating for a move away from annuals, we're not suggesting that you abandon them entirely. In fact, we love using annuals as accents throughout the year — it can be as simple as adding pansies and herbs in the spring; tiny, delicately drooping begonias in summer; or unusual greens such as tatsoi (*Brassica rapa*) or 'Red Bor' kale (*Brassica oleracea*) in fall. Or it can be more visually arresting by adding a bright pink million bells (*Calibrachoa*) or rusty orange gloriosa daisies (*Rudbeckia hirta*). Take your pick: the annuals world is large and vibrantly colored.

We like to use a good amount of cut plant materials, especially during the holiday season. We love the branches of red- or yellow-berried hollies like winterberry (*Ilex verticillata*), and dogwood (*Cornus stolonifera*) or corkscrew hazel sticks (*Corylus avellana* 'Contorta'), as well as all the more traditional greens and pinecones. We'll also hang all manner of things from the branches of our potted specimens including glass icicles, birdseed ornaments, fuzzy blobs of mossy lichens, and of course lights, all the way until spring.

of them to be a flowering tree that balances heft with delicacy. We chose a magnolia (*Magnolia*). The house with which we paired it is a lovely, mansard-roofed farmhouse that sits on a quiet country road lined with mature oaks, maples, and sycamores that overhang the few cars that pass by. The house has a porch and a deep pinky red door. The girly pink spring blossoms, lush blowsy green foliage of summer, golden fall color, and soft gray bark and fuzzy pearly green buds of winter made a perfect match with the house. A container based on the woodland feel of birch (*Betula*) or the heft of an oakleaf hydrangea (*Hydrangea quercifolia*) wouldn't have suited this sweet house and its family quite as well.

Using these basic reference points, head to the nursery and start browsing. With this method, you can start any time of the year. For the purposes of the book, we started when the gardening season tradition-ally begins in the Northeast — spring! Starting this project in the early autumn, however, is also excellent, because you can visit the nursery when things are quiet and plants may be less expensive. You also have an opportunity to see plants doing what they do in fall. If you decide to select a single back-bone plant, you want to make sure that it has something more to it than pretty spring flowers. If you pick a plant for its spar-kling fall attributes, chances are you'll be delighted come spring.

The surrounding grassy marshland inspired our grass-and-perennial-based container.

21

GET THEE TO A NURSERY

The very first thing we recommend is finding the best nursery in your area, particularly if you are a relatively new gardener. Buying plants online can be fun and exhilarating but also intimidating and a challenge if you're not sure what you're looking for. A high-quality nursery is valuable in so many ways. It can take some time to find, but it's worth driving a good distance to find one. You wouldn't choose a couch just because it's the only one available close to your house, would you? When we go to a nursery, we judge it on two levels — the quality of its plants and the knowledge and helpfulness of the staff.

The importance of selecting a well-grown, balanced, healthy plant from the get-go can't be overstated. At left, Sara is holding a compact, evenly leafed and branched oakleaf hydrangea. The lopsided, uneven growth of Roanne's specimen makes it a poor choice for a container planting.

The Plant (Health and) Beauty Contest

When you're out shopping at the nursery, don't just settle for any old plant. Take your time, pull plants out of line, judge them like you would a beauty contest. To find the best plant of the bunch, start by looking at the foliage, as it's an important indicator of a plant's health. Provided the plant you're looking at has broken its winter dormancy, the leaves should be out and have a rich color that's appropriate to its variety (for example, some plants are bred to have light green foliage; on other plants, this is a sign of nutrient deficiency). Plants that have small, chewed, torn, puckered, or mottled leaves should be left at the nursery. A plant's foliage should be clean, free of insects, and evenly developed on all sides of the specimen.

Another important indicator — one that can be a bit trickier to check out — is root health and development. If you want to look at a plant's roots before buying, ask a nursery person; he or she should be happy to help you. With perennials, it's fine to see a little bit of root poking out the bottom of the pot. When you're purchasing trees, it's especially important to make sure the roots are healthy. You want to avoid both the tree that has too little growth and won't transplant well and the one that's been in the same container so long it has thick roots circling the pot.

For both trees and shrubs, an opening of any kind in the bark is an open door for disease and possibly death. Check to make sure the trunk is not damaged; that branches are not cracked, split, or rubbing against each other; and that the plant has an even, open canopy. This all takes extra time, but it's worth the trouble.

We like to buy our plants in containers (as opposed to balled and burlapped, which is a more common way to find the bigger shrubs and trees); we find that they are happier to be transplanted, perhaps because they've already settled into container life at the nursery. The only downside is that they could have settled into container life all *too* well. If a plant has been in a container too long without attention, it can become root-bound. This is when the roots start to circle around and around the container, with nowhere else to go. Not good. If a plant seems big for its container, ask someone from the nursery to check out the roots for you, to make sure it's not pot-bound.

Helpful Nursery Staff

At a good nursery or garden center, knowledgeable, helpful staff members will often guide you to the coolest plants, and they can help you pick out the best plant of a group. They're familiar with the plants because they work with them every day. They can also advise you on the best way to take care of a plant's needs — they're like walking encyclopedias. Some plant tags are misleading, but a good nursery staff member will make sure you don't end up with a plant that won't do well for you in the spot you have in mind for it. Sometimes the owner herself is there. Almost all of our favorite nurseries and garden centers are ones where the owners are on-site most of the time (see Resources, page 258, for some of our favorites).

Selecting Good Backbone Perennials for Containers

WHEN SELECTING A PERENNIAL that will make a good backbone plant, there are a few important elements to consider. The first thing to remember is that perennials die back to the ground during the winter months, so this means you will need to make up for that in the early spring and winter with other plants that evoke the feeling of the perennial-to-be or with a planting that is compatible with the resting perennial.

Think about structure of the plant, as that will dictate the feel of the entire composition. Is it vase-shaped? Tall and slender? Broad and beefy?

Next think about foliage — its color, texture, shape, and size. If you are making a planting around a fern, choose one that is visually hefty and eye-catching; not all of them are delicate little forest dwellers.

Will your perennial offer seasonal or year-round interest? Bear in mind that you want this plant to be providing interest for as long as possible, so try not to think about its flowers as the main selling point. Or if you love its flower — as we love coneflowers (*Echinacea*)— find out if it blooms for a long period of time and if it has pretty seedheads.

Does this perennial require staking? Since these container plantings are quite small compared with what might be a more typical garden bed, try to stay away from plants that need staking, unless you want to add an ornamental structure of some kind that could both hold up your plants and be decorative.

Coneflowers (*Echinacea*) make excellent backbone perennials and come in a vast array of colors.

All this said, nurseries can be busy places, especially during spring, so finding someone to guide you in your search for the perfect plants might not be possible every time. Shopping during the weekdays is always a good bet for finding a quieter time, or even in the evenings after work (nurseries are often open until 6 or 7 during the spring and summer). If you can't do a weekday, try to get to the nursery as early in the day as you can on a weekend.

We probably annoy nursery sales staff when we're working on our underplantings. We're always creating little piles of plants in various sections of the nursery as we shop. We stop, gather a fun texture, and pair it with another plant. Two rows later we find yet another plant, maybe one we like better, and we combine the piles and make some decisions. The more experimenting you can do in the nursery sales yard the better! This exercise is really helpful — it shows you what your options are, gives you insight for future seasonal plantings, and leads you to a Plan B to fall back on in the case of a plant revolt or death.

It's fun to make little combinations on the ground at the nursery when you're trying to decide what to buy. Just be sure to put whatever plants you don't buy back where they belong!

Pushing the Envelope

When you're looking at plants, try to push yourself beyond your usual choices, but be realistic at the same time. Sara has been in her current garden for five years now, and for about four and half of those years, she fooled herself into thinking part of it was sunny. Of course, then she was disappointed with the performance of the catmint (*Nepeta*), the peonies (*Paeonia*), and the sunflowers (*Helianthus*). Once she was honest with herself and her garden — it is a shade garden — she adjusted her plantings and has been much more satisfied with it and enjoyed everything about it much more. So save yourself the time and truly look at what you have.

Our Favorite Plant Themes

FOR THE 12 CONTAINER PLANTINGS IN THIS BOOK, we tried to home in on a particular attribute or theme that inspired us; some focus on a single plant, some on a group of plants. We made our choices in order to help gardeners think about the range of attributes that are available.

Japanese maples often have exquisite bark, another exciting attribute of this great plant.

Here are the 12 we chose and why we chose them:

COLORFUL STICKS (YELLOWTWIG DOGWOOD) — Adding sticks and twigs to winter containers has become *de rigueur* in the garden-design world, and for good reason. They bring texture, height, color, and movement to any design. Why add sticks to a container when you can just grow them in it? With both yellowtwig and redtwig dogwood, you'll be growing your own stick supply for other compositions when you eventually plant out the shrub into the garden.

COOL BARK (BIRCH) — Because the two of us live in a cold-winter region, we particularly like trees and shrubs that have elements of beauty year-round. Beautiful bark is one of the best elements, because it covers much of the tree and can be quite eye-catching. We chose birch because it has magical parchment-paper-like layers of cream-colored bark. It also has slender, delicate branches with little catkin earrings in spring. In autumn, the almost translucent leaves turn a clear yellow.

OFF-SEASON BLOOMER — We love plants that shine at unusual times like the autumn crocus (*Colchicum autumnale*), autumn cherry (*Prunus subhirtellus* 'Autumnalis'), and even Swiss chard (*Beta vulgaris* var. *cicla*) used in spring plantings. They provide an element of surprise in the garden that often brings a smile. The plant we've used to highlight this is a summer-blooming azalea (*Rhododendron*). It blooms in early summer (an unusual time for azaleas); has fragrant, vibrant flowers; and sports leaves that are a lovely matte blue-green.

Evergreen topiaries add the perfect touch of formality to any garden.

FORMAL EVERGREEN (BOXWOOD TOPIARY) — Evergreen topiaries are classics and can be added to just ever so slightly to make them even more exquisite than they already are. They can be one of the most adaptable plants to a variety of sites. Boxwood is the most classic choice for this type of planting.

SPRING-BLOOMING SHRUB (FOTHERGILLA) — We really love adding shrubs to the garden (and containers) that have all-season appeal. At first glance, it can be hard to find ones that have both fragrant spring blooms and gorgeous crisp foliage that twinkles with color in the autumn. Fothergilla fits the bill, with its chartreuse buds and young leaves, stellar fall foliage, and interesting branch structure that's perfect for a container.

Purple foliage is particularly beguiling in a container garden, because it works well with a range of other colors, from silver to red.

COLORFUL FOLIAGE (BURGUNDY JAPANESE MAPLE) — We love plants with purple foliage! The end. If you love plants with gray foliage, screaming chartreuse, or crazy variegation, why not make it the theme of the whole container planting?

SHADE-LOVING SHRUB (OAKLEAF HYDRANGEA) —
Just as we love shrubs that sing in more than one season in the sun, we love shrubs that shine in the shade. They help those of us who lack that sunny southern exposure by adding structure to shade gardens that may be lush and happy with perennials. Oakleaf hydrangea has large, dimensional, dynamic blossoms in summer; big broad leaves that turn deep berry shades in the autumn; and cool cinnamon bark in the winter.

SPRING-FLOWERING TREE (MAGNOLIA) — Who doesn't love pulling down a branch loaded with blooms to drink in the fragrance or to get immersed in the rich colors of spring blossom? We especially love a tree that has super-girly pink and white blooms in spring, fuzzy buds that mingle happily with the yellow leaves in fall, and an intricate branch structure that is elegant in winter.

BERRY BEAUTIFUL (BLUEBERRY) — The range of berried shrubs is wide, and you shouldn't stop at just one. The colorful berries will often last through the fall, adding even more color to an already lovely season. Blueberries are treasured by birds and humans alike, and the red fall foliage is pretty great, too. We also love the mahogany color of the branches.

A FAMILY OF TRANSPLANTS (PERENNIALS) — We used sun-loving perennials because they're widely available, easily transplanted to (and from) the garden, and their range of color and textures is virtually unlimited.

SEASIDE MOVEMENT (GRASSES AND COMPANY) —
Grasses are a great backbone for any container. They play well with many other plants, they can be cast in many different roles, and they change with the season. We used chives (to evoke the feeling of grasses before they had come up), sedges (*Carex*), and switchgrass (*Panicum*).

STRUCTURE AND VINES (BAMBOO TEPEE) —

Structure in the garden is essential; it adds an element of permanence and height that might be lacking otherwise. Man-made supports — such as obelisks, lattice, and tepees — allow the gardener to bring ornament into the garden in a subtle, pretty way. Vines do the same thing, although providing even more height if allowed to scramble up beyond their structure. A bamboo tepee is a classic, easy, inexpensive way to highlight and support vines of all kinds. It's not permanent but is very versatile — you get a good structure without a lot of commitment.

Sadly, not all berries are edible for humans, but they do lend a sparkle of crimson, salmon, lavender, and scarlet to the waning growing season.

29

Handle Carefully

Roanne is gently clearing soil from the top of the root ball, avoiding the main feeder roots of the maple, so she can begin on the underplanting.

PERENNIALS WITH HEFTY TAPROOTS and fragile surface roots or runners are tricky to transplant. Whether in the container or in the garden, these finicky friends want to move in and stay put, so if you'd like to use them in a container combination, they'll need a little extra care.

First of all, be sure to start with a new container-grown plant rather than one that's been growing in the ground; its root system will be more self-contained and used to living in cramped quarters. Take care when removing the plant from its grow pot. And for the best chance at success, remove as little soil from the roots as possible.

Here are a few examples of the more fragile (read: needy) plants.

Perennials with taproots: wand flower (*Gaura*), false indigo (*Baptisia*), Queen Anne's lace (*Daucus carota*), oriental poppy (*Papaver orientale*), Russian sage (*Perovskia atriplicifolia*), butterfly weed (*Asclepias tuberosa*), lupine (*Lupinus*), and larkspur (*Consolida ajacis*)

Perennials with fragile surface roots: bleeding heart (*Dicentra*), columbine (*Aquilegia*), and most ferns

We used sweet white daffodils, periwinkle (*Vinca minor*), violets (*Viola*), ferns, bugleweed (*Ajuga reptans*), and others. Even the color palette supported the calming feeling that we wanted to create with soft purple, cream, silver, and dark purple.

However, if Mr. Birch had been planted in an über-modern setting in a sleek zinc vessel, then we would have selected underplants that sup-port and enhance that feeling and look. You would want to keep things simple and clean. To achieve this level of simplic-ity, you could underplant with a grouping of just one kind of fern or a monochromatic selec-tion of silvery woodlanders such as Japanese painted fern (*Athyrium nipponicum* 'Ghost'), bugloss (*Brunnera* 'Jack Frost'), and dead nettle (*Lamium* 'Silver Nancy'). They should be the fun, frilly accessories full of texture and interesting color. You want your combinations to be inter-esting yet flow happily together.

Inspiration is everywhere! Look at your favorite garden combinations or in garden pub-lications. Get ideas from a floral arrangement or a beautifully garnished dinner plate; color and texture are everywhere. Make note of what you like and make it work for you.

CONTAINERS ARE YOUR CARDIGANS

We like the phrase "containers are your cardigans" because containers can (and should!) be used in any garden, of any style and any size. Their effect can change depending on where you place them and the plants you put inside them, just as a little cashmere cardigan can be thrown over a summer beach dress to fend off the morning ocean chill or worn over a sassy little black dress on your way to a fancy wedding. Your containers can be this way, too. And just as cardigans are, in our opinion, a necessary part of any wardrobe, containers of some kind or another are a necessary part of any garden. So, black, navy, beige, wool, cotton, polyester, cable knit, V-neck — take your pick. Terra-cotta, composite, zinc, concrete, gray, brown, black, square, round, tall, short — choose your vessel.

Practical Matters

It is hard to know which container to choose, so how do you narrow it down, given all the choices available? And there are both practical and design considerations as well. On a practical level, there are three major aspects to consider when choosing a container: cost, durability, and weight. Perhaps cost should be tackled first, since for most of us, it will help narrow down the choices. That said, don't cheap out — a

The range of containers is vast — in material, color, shape, and size — leaving you open to choose whatever suits your fancy. Because we like to select our main plant first, we often use that plant as well as our home's style to dictate which container we choose.

Choosing a Central Plant and Container

Pick your plant because:

• You love it entirely and inexplicably or you love one of its attributes.

• Because the plant works in your space from a design standpoint (or both of the above).

Once you have the plant selected, pick the vessel:

• Does the plant fit into it?

• Do the material and shape suit your location, design-wise? (Is your house modern? Cottage-y? World-style? Classic? Woodsy?)

• Do you live where there is frost? Yes or no? (If yes: you can choose from concrete, zinc, wood, and composite. If no: choose from the above, plus terra-cotta and glazed terra-cotta.)

• Does it fit your budget?

A sturdy cement container weighs a ton but can stay out through the winter. Terra-cotta is gorgeous but fragile.

container should be viewed as an investment. Buy the best-quality container you can afford and take care of it. If you buy a big, relatively cheap terra-cotta container for your composition and you leave it out through the winter, we guarantee it will be cracked before winter has even settled in. So while it was inexpensive at the start, the cost will just add up as you buy replacements. As far as initial cost goes, terra-cotta and polycarbonate composite or resin containers tend to be the least expensive, whereas stone and concrete containers tend to be the most expensive. The bottom line is that if you're on a budget, don't hesitate to use high-quality composite containers; they look great and the cost is reasonable when you factor in the length of time you'll own them.

The next consideration is durability, which is determined by the material. Any container, from concrete to cast iron to composite, can and will break down over time, but will do so at very different rates.

If you live somewhere that freezes in winter — which is the case for both of us —you need

This oakleaf hydrangea (*Hydrangea quercifolia*) is roughly twice the size of the container: a good balance of proportions.

to bring terra-cotta and glazed-ceramic containers into a frost-free place where they will be protected from the elements; the garage and the basement both work well. Conversely, concrete and stone are incredibly durable, taking the seasons' shifts in temperature and water in stride and gaining a beautiful patina all the while.

Bear in mind that durability often comes with a cost — both literally and figuratively. More-durable containers will come with a higher price tag. Also, concrete, stone, and cast-iron

containers weigh a *lot*. This is something to bear in mind when you're selecting a vessel. Do you like to move your plantings around? Do you change your mind frequently? If so, you're better off choosing a lightweight container or you'll put yourself in traction. Keeping these considerations in mind, you then might head to the nursery and begin selecting your vessel.

Choosing a Container from a Design Perspective

Should you pick your plant or container first? If we were working with annuals, we would confidently say container first . . . go ahead, buy the mossy, aged Italian terra-cotta heartthrob you've been eyeing, fill it with gorgeous geraniums, and smile in pleasure. If your geraniums happen to mold or you forget to make watering arrangements while you vacation in August, toss out the plants and try again — maybe this time a party of ornamental veggies. Whichever plants you decide on, Signore Terra-cotta will make it all right.

This logic, however, just doesn't work with these staple trees and shrubs. It doesn't work for three reasons:

The health of the plant. You just acquired a lovely birch (*Betula*) — and trees, shrubs, and perennials cost more than a 4-inch annual — shouldn't it be happy? You'll need to provide plenty of depth, great drainage, and room to have underplantings. Make sure you select a vessel that will accommodate the needs of your staple plant.

The visual subtlety of the planting. Harmony of the whole is important. Just like the frame of a picture, the vessel plays an integral part in the overall composition.

The long-term commitment. Sometimes a staple plant stays in for a year. Sometimes, like in the case of a boxwood (*Buxus*) topiary or a birch, it can stay longer. Certain vessels overwinter well, whereas others don't. Containers come in many materials, shapes, and sizes. Be sure to select one whose construction is able to hold up to the environment you live in.

Once you select the staple plant and have determined the

Containers Dictate Style

TRY TO DISTILL THE BASIC DESIGN QUALITIES of your home and your neighborhood or the land around you. Listen to the language you have created for your home or garden. Over the years, you've surrounded yourself with all sorts of materials, colors, and flavors. Your vessel will feel more grounded and will cast a satisfying, comfortable feeling onto your plants if you select a vessel style that is consistent with you and your surroundings. You don't have to pair modern with modern all the time; traditional and modern can work, global style and minimalism can pair nicely, too. Successfully marry plant to vessel, vessel to site, and you will achieve a look that is both stylish and full of originality.

TRADITIONAL

• Charming simplicity, Shaker farmhouse, Beacon Hill brownstone, shingled weathered house.

• Gives cozy feelings and connects us to the past by using familiar styles from previous generations.

• Beams, whitewash, shingles, patinas. Aged mossy items, familiar shapes and materials.

• Pale chalky colors, aged wood, brick, cobblestone.

• *Traditional Home* magazine, Martha Stewart, Restoration Hardware.

• English garden, boxwood, aged woods.

• Concrete vessels in classic shapes, aged moss terra-cotta or stone, metals with patina.

CONTEMPORARY/MINIMAL

• Clean lines and simple shapes and forms. The intentional use of color. Gropius, Eames, and Rothko.

• The absence of clutter gives you room to breathe. Objects are intentionally placed and are individual works of art.

• Concrete, natural fibers, polyethylene, zinc, stainless steel, glass with limited framing, sleek lighting, great typography.

• Design Within Reach, *Dwell* magazine, Helvetica, Herman Miller.

• Grasses, succulents and agave, ground covers, massed plantings for a big statement.

• Zinc vessels, galvanized vessels, modern whiskey barrel, clean wooden vessels, fiberglass cubes.

GLOBAL STYLE

• Travel inspired. Interpretations and adaptations of elements from other cultures. Tiki huts, Asian-inspired outdoor spaces.

• A tribal, indigenous feel that lends itself to a peppery, spice-toned palette. Objects may be travel souvenirs. Sensuous, exotic.

• Richly patterned materials, brass, ceramic, bamboo, statuary.

• Pier One, Landry and Acari, *National Geographic*.

• Exotic-looking plants, grasses, bamboo.

• Glazed ceramic pots, bronzed vessels, dried sisal vessels, Vietnamese water jugs.

COTTAGE STYLE

• Light, breezy, informal, weathered. Vintage chic. Light colors. Informal pairings and imperfect floors. Warm fun accessories make cozy spaces. Recycled materials, hand-me-down treasures. Clean fonts. Nice watering cans, Arts and Crafts Movement, bungalow inspired, William Morris.

• Slipcovered sofas, beachy palettes, painted floors.

• Pottery Barn, *Cottage Living* magazine (if only it were still around!), Anthropologie.

• Simple plants with emotional meaning, blossoms.

• French oil jars, Italian terra-cotta, galvanized feed troughs, concrete in simple forms with a texture.

style of the site (see page 21), use this information to decide the style of your container. Will the planting be living in your modern portico or will it be resting in front of a shingled facade in the woods?

Appearance and Texture

The individual vessel does influence how you view the whole composition. A container may make your birch planting feel rustic, contemporary, or relaxed. Ideally, the style of your container will also complement the mood of your space, though you shouldn't feel obliged to stick with one particular style.

Be open and experiment. Harmony should be your mantra. Think about the colors and textures of the vessel and how it casts a mood. Patinas and aged or distressed vessels give a sense of depth and complement the fresh, lively feeling the plants give off.

Proportion

The appearance and texture are not the only qualities to be concerned with — harmony of proportions is important, too. When matching a vessel to a plant, try to make sure the following is also in check:

Plant elements and container should have some feature in common. Birch bark has a patina-like feel, creamy and modern, as does our pale gray concrete vessel.

Is It a Vessel or a Container?

SARA AND I TALK ABOUT THIS A LOT. Vessel or container? We both call planting in a vessel "container gardening" and call the end result a "contained garden." Then why do I feel so compelled to call the item in which our plants are contained a "vessel"? The term has its flaws. It does sometimes evoke a feeling of contained liquid, like a blood vessel or an ocean vessel. Nonetheless, I think I call it this because to me a vessel holds love and spirit, whereas a container holds chips and dishwasher soap.

Vessel gives me the feeling of permanence. Containers can be recycled and tossed away. These structures are more solid and cherished, so they need a special name.　— Roanne

I TEND TO USE THE WORD *CONTAINER*, well, because that's what it does: it contains the plants and the soil in one spot. It is what differentiates this type of gardening from gardening in the ground. Roanne uses the word *vessel* and, of course, once Roanne started telling me why she uses vessel instead of container, I sort of changed my mind. But I still have a hard time pushing the word out of my mouth. So I use the word *container*, even though it now sort of makes me think I'm gardening in take-out Chinese-food boxes. Oh well. *Vessel* seems kind of loaded for what we're doing here. But maybe it's not! Gardening is important and a vessel has solid, permanent connotations.　— Sara

The height of the staple plant or central element should be in balance with the size of the vessel. Avoid selecting a plant that is exactly the same size as the vessel; equal parts can quickly become visually monotonous. Try working in thirds, making the plant either one-third or two-thirds the size of the vessel. If the vessel looks visually heavy, try selecting a plant that is two or three times the height of the container.

The vessel should also be in proportion to its surroundings. For example, imagine you're creating a planting at the entrance to your house. The vessel shouldn't be dwarfed by the doorway, nor should it overwhelm the entrance. The planting itself should effortlessly fit into the environment; it should look like it's always been there. After all, you want your guests to admire your gorgeous combination, not be distracted by the placement of the vessel or by a planting that's out of proportion. The only thing you want your guests to think about when they interact with the planting is "Wow! This container rocks!"

Don't Forget the Drainage!

Providing the right amount of water is one of the most important keys to success in container gardening. The best way to make sure you give your planting the right amount is to first check that the container you choose has enough holes in the bottom to let the excess water drain away. This may seem counterintuitive — why would I want the all-important water to drain away?

Well, here's the thing: your plants need water, but too much could cause the roots of a plant to rot and then, well, the plant will die. So, water your container until the water is freely running out the bottom. Then you will know that enough water has been absorbed by the soil to satisfy the plants but that the excess is draining away.

Make sure that your container has drainage holes and has *enough* of them. More than once, we've looked into a container, thought we'd seen the drainage holes, and then wondered why our plant was drowning in muck two months later. It is worth filling your empty container a quarter full with water before you plant it. Watch how quickly — or slowly — the water comes out. If it is just coming out in a trickle, add an extra hole or two. Most containers made for plants have enough.

Generally, terra-cotta, glazed ceramic, concrete, and stone have one large central drainage hole. This is enough because these materials also allow water to seep through the sides of the container — very slowly. Polycarbonate composite and metal containers are less forgiving and may need extra holes drilled in, as the drainage holes are the only way that water can escape. For example, with the brown plastic container we use for our Japanese maple planting, we drilled several extra holes just to be sure the water could get out.

If there are no drainage holes in your favorite container, you can drill some before you plant in it. Depending on the material — composites and metals may need more — start with two holes and run some water through the container.

If you think the water is still moving too slowly, drill three more. To begin, drill with the smallest drill bit and go slowly. If you are drilling into ceramic or concrete, you may need to get a drill bit from the hardware store that is specific to the material. A standard drill bit and too much force can cause cracking.

Sometimes the surface you want to place your container on is very flat and even — good for you. In this case, though, this lovely surface can essentially block drainage. You can find "feet" or small trivets in a range of materials and sizes, but they all do the same job — they elevate your container ever so slightly off the ground, allowing enough clearance for proper drainage.

How to Drill a Drainage Hole

1. Turn the container upside down and place it on a secure surface.
2. Use a nail or a screwdriver tip to make a small nick where you want to drill the hole. This helps prevent the bit from slipping and cracking any decorative glaze or paint.
3. Choose your drill bit. Use a tile or ceramic drill bit for glazed containers, concrete, and terra-cotta. A standard twist drill bit works well on zinc, galvanized metal, wooden, and composite vessels.
4. We like to start small with a 3/16-inch bit. Drill a hole by placing the bit into the nick you made on the base of the container. Make sure that the drill bit is straight up and down. Press down firmly on the drill and then drill through the base of the container in a steady, single motion. If you are unsure of drainage-hole size, we recommend making a first "pilot hole" and then using larger bits as needed. The pilot hole keeps the drill from jumping around and reduces heat, which may cause a container to crack.
5. Remove any dust or metal particles and sand lightly; you don't want sharp edges to cut your fingers!

PLANTING UP AND SWAPPING OUT

How you plant up — that is, physically put your plants into your container — is one of the most critical steps in achieving a happy and lush container design. There are things that are the same or similar to planting in the ground and things that are quite different. Because the habitat, and in particular the soil, is completely enclosed and therefore completely dependent on the gardener for its well-being, you have to take special care to get it right from the get-go.

Don't Treat Your Soil Like Dirt

It is always a bit of a bummer that both *soil* and *dirt* often have such negative connotations in the English language; words that come up first in the dictionary relate them to filth, worthlessness, corruption, and worse. Of course, gardeners never think of dirt in this way, since most gardeners do what they do because of a very

physical need to get their hands back in (or keep them in) the dirt. Gardening, and with it the requisite and delightful soil handling, puts us back in direct touch with the earth and the natural world in a way that can be hard to come by these days. We call it *soil*, that substance we plant into, whether it's on the ground or in a container. The word *medium* could work, too, but it just seems too ghostly to us and not close enough to the soil that lies outside in our gardens.

The first thing to know is that it is important to start with good soil. The ideal container soil must be lightweight and porous enough to drain well, but not too porous. It should be high enough in organic matter to retain water and feed the plants. Soil straight from the garden shouldn't be used because it won't drain fast enough, which translates into too little air for the roots. Generally speaking, we buy our potting soil, and we buy it from companies that use organic components and sustainable practices. Among our favorites are Coast of Maine and Vermont Compost Company.

Roanne mixes good rich potting soil with a dose of perlite to ensure good drainage.

We both prefer to use organic potting soil in containers — one that comes without synthetic fertilizers. Planting up a container means handling soil, and we've both had skin reactions to some kinds of nonorganic potting soils. Plus, we have children and pets about and prefer to keep our gardens as chemical-free as possible. There are many excellent soils that have compost or shrimp shells or leaf mold added, so we'll go for those when we can.

Most commercially grown plants contain a fair amount of fertilizers already. (Have a close look while you're planting things up in your big container. If you see little yellow, green, or brownish pellets or balls, they are almost certainly fertilizer.) Because you're adding new plants to the container every season, you're inevitably adding a bit of nutrients with the new soil you put in to fill in the gaps and tuck around the new additions. This little bit of fertilizer is the perfect amount for the staple plant to continue making new roots and producing beautiful leaves, flowers, and fruits.

Making Your Own Mix

SOME GARDENERS PREFER TO MIX their own potting soil, because they like knowing exactly what's in it. Also, it enables them to tailor the mix to the plants they are growing. You might find you'd like to do the same, particularly if you're growing plants that need soil a bit more on the acid side, for example, like blueberries and azaleas. Ro sometimes takes a store-bought mix and lightens it up with perlite or vermiculite. It's also a good idea to add a bit of compost to increase the soil's fertility.

PLANTING UP YOUR CONTAINER

When commercial nurseries propagate plants for sale, they either grow them in nursery pots or cultivate them in the ground (these are called "field-grown"). Field-grown trees and shrubs are dug up when they reach a salable size, and the root balls are wrapped in burlap; this process is sometimes referred to by nursery folks as "B&B," for "balled-and-burlapped." We prefer to use plants that have been grown in containers, rather than those that have been field grown, because we've found that containerized plants are already accustomed to life in a pot and adjust to their new container setting more readily. We also find that containerized plants are often more manicured than field-grown plants are.

When planting into containers, treat the roots of your plant as gently as possible. If the plant has spent a considerable amount of time growing in a container at the nursery, you'll need to check the root ball for circulating roots and gently straighten them out. (Even though a well-grown plant may not be totally root-bound — a situation where the big roots of the plants are doing laps around the container and form a tight, messy, snarl — its roots may be starting to make circular patterns.) You'll also want to make sure that you're planting your tree or shrub upright, not listing to one side. Be careful not to bury the trunk, and orient the tree with its best face to the world.

Planting a Tree or Shrub in a Container

At this point, you've chosen where your container will sit and you will want to set up the container on its feet if that is something you found was needed to help with drainage.

Remove the tree/shrub from the container or burlap wrapping (if you've bought a balled-and-burlapped plant). Assess the root ball and consider what needs to be done to make the plant fit into its container. Ideally, you will have purchased a vessel large enough to accommodate the tree without chipping away too much of the roots. Sometimes

41

INITIAL UNDER-PLANTING

Like so many people, we like to plant containers for instant gratification. And because we swap out plants with the season, we're able to maintain the look and feel of that initial planting. To achieve a lush, full

The backbone plant should sit low in the container, so that underplantings can be stacked onto the root ball.

look right off the bat, we pack a lot of plants into one vessel. We may stack a plant on top of another plant's root ball, build up a mound and plant into it, or tuck the smallest plants or bulbs into the root ball of a larger plant. Anything is game, as long as roots are covered and water is accessible. Circulation is important, drainage is important, adequate light is important; covering your plant's roots is *crucial*. If a plant's roots don't get covered with soil — their source for water and food— they will dry out quickly. This will cause a quick decline for the plant, one from which it is difficult to recover. If you can't get soil on them immediately, even a covering of damp moss or mulch is better than exposing roots to the air.

Most of the underplantings will stay in the container for a season or two, then it's off to the garden, where they can thrive in their ideal environment. Underplantings that stay in the vessel longer usually do so because they are rock stars: they're thriving or have just exceeded our expectations, so we leave them in.

Swapping Out the Underplantings

When it comes time to swap out the initial underplantings, start by assessing what will stay, what will move on, and what you need to buy. The best way to tell if it is time to move in another plant is whether the prime-time season of the perennial or shrub you were using is past and there is no second season. Some plants — such as heucheras (*Heuchera*), epimediums (*Epimedium*), hosta (*Hosta*), lady's mantle (*Alchemilla*), or lamb's ear (*Stachys*) — hold up through the seasons and can stay in a container. Others, like pansies, herbs, miniature roses, and most bulbs, need to come out, because they get too long and gangly or just stop blooming and don't offer another special characteristic. Sometimes a plant will take off, sprout a baby, get a bit leggy; you just need to embrace the spontaneity and adapt. Or maybe it's time to shift gears, trim the plant, transplant something out, or head to the nursery for its replacement. A 4-inch ground cover needs to be moundy and great in the tenth of the vessel space we've

By the end of a season, some plants maybe begin to look a bit leggy and spent; that's when you know it is time to swap out your planting.

Some plants (like the ivy in this container) can be left in with just a little tidying up; others need to be replaced with plants that offer more of a seasonal spark, like these pink roses.

allotted — that's all. If it grows all big and crazy, we divide it and plant it over in the walkway. Giddy-up!

We like to buy our new additions a week to a few days before we plan to transplant. You can buy them the day of planting, but sometimes it is nice to spend some extra time contemplating their placement and then sleep on it before you put them in the vessels. This is not to say that you can't move them around while planting, but the less you harass your new plant friends, the better and faster they will rebound from their move. Ro will often swap out plants one day and place the new additions — still in their pots — on top of the remaining container planting to get a feel for where things might go when she actually plants them a few days later.

Timing and Preparation

In the days before you do a plant swap, tidy up your container, give plants that have grown a bit long and leggy a little haircut, and make sure the container is well watered. In an ideal world, the plants going into the container should get water a few days before the transplanting too, or the morning of if the day is very warm. You want all the plants coming out of the container and going into the container to be minimally stressed. You probably don't want to water your container immediately before planting and transplanting, just so it doesn't turn into a sloppy, muddy mess.

The best kind of day to transplant is a cool, cloudy one. If you can't get the weather to cooperate, transplant in the coolest, shadiest spot in your garden and work in the morning or evening. If you can't do that, then for the plants' sake, water the container well and keep a close eye on things for the week following the transplanting.

Swapping out. First things first. Assuming you started off with good, rich soil and watered your plants enough to keep them happy, the telltale result will be lush roots, leaves, and stems tangled together in a happy, blowsy combination. Gingerly, using your hands (bare is best for this work) or a slender digging tool, such as a hori-hori (a Japanese farmer's knife), pry and pull the plants out of the container. Try to bring as much soil and root ball with them as you can. It's best to have a space in the garden ready for your transplants. But the best of ideas often go off-track, so what we usually do is

have empty containers and soil ready to receive our transplants. We pot them up, give them a good drink of water, and set them aside until we're ready to figure out where they'll go in the garden. Sometimes, if the plants coming out of the big container still look great, you can pot them up on their own and display them for a bit with the container as it transitions into the next season.

Preparing the container to receive its new friends. When planting in conjunction with one large plant — such as a tree or shrub — serving as the backbone, we often scratch a fair bit of soil off the top of the root ball, about 2 inches. You can do this with your hands or a small handheld cultivator. Start with a firm hand, but then go easy when you begin to see the fine, hairlike roots and then the larger side roots. These are ones you want to avoid damaging, the larger side roots being the ones that support the plant and provide the main source of transport for water and nutrients to the rest of the plant.

Swapping in. Begin planting from the outer edge of the

We took this lovely little piggyback plant out of our magnolia container, potted him up, and turned him into a houseplant.

pot up to the trunk or base of the backbone plant. You can remove a significant amount of soil from the new plants in order to fit them in, but start with removing as little as possible, slowly taking off more soil and roots as necessary. As you plant them in the container, be sure to firm in plants and fill in all air pockets with extra soil. It's worth planting, filling with soil, watering, then returning a few hours later to fill in with more soil where plants have settled.

Positioning. Try not to position underplantings in unnatural orientations. Yes, you can tweak a plant; maybe it needs a little push so it will cascade out of the vessel. But please don't tilt a quart-size cotoneaster so that it's nearly resting on its side just to soften the edge of the planting. Look at how your garden bed and its denizens evolve together. You do not have mini-conifers growing up over your coneflowers. It's nice to push limits, but try to keep to what happens naturally.

There is no magic number as to how many plants we obtain, but odd numbers are always best. The key is balance, interest, and unity. Your eye wants to take in the whole at first, then travel to all the individual plants and enjoy what each one has to offer. The plant you're gazing at should lead you off to another portion of the planting, whether through perceived motion, color, or texture.

Swapping In Transplants from Your Garden

A GREAT SOURCE OF PLANTS for your underplantings is your very own garden. Many healthy perennials spread or clump up to a size much too big for their original space. Take advantage of this; spread the wealth into your container. If you have lamb's ear (*Stachys*) or lady's mantle (*Alchemilla*) in your garden, dig up some of it and use it in your containers.

In order to have the transplant be in top shape when it goes into your container, you should give the plant a few days' rest in its own pot, so that it can bounce back from transplant shock (it may wilt and pout, but it will recover in a couple of days). Some plants may not make it, but most will thrive. Experiment and have fun!

Here's a step-by-step plan for getting your transplants off to a good start:

• Water the plant to be swapped in on the day before you plan to transplant it. This ensures that the whole plant will be hydrated when it's time to dig.

• Find a temporary home for your transplant (we often reuse plastic nursery pots for this).

• Water the plant both before and after planting it into its temporary home. Soak the root ball so that the soil will adhere to the roots and keep them moist.

• Ideally, wait three days to let the plant stabilize. Shield it from direct sunlight. Make sure the roots are covered with soil.

• Place the transplant into your container composition. Be even gentler with it than you would with a container-grown plant.

• Lightly firm the soil around the transplant.

• Water with the rest of the container.

47

CARING FOR YOUR CONTAINED GARDEN

Maintenance throughout the year is important for any container planting. But whereas a vessel filled with annuals may need constant fertilizing and deadheading to keep plants looking their best, with our technique you're dealing mostly with perennials and shrubs, which, by their very nature, are relatively low maintenance. Also, we like to think that each time you swap out plants for a new season, you get an opportunity to interact with the planting in a way that makes caring for it convenient and enjoyable. Sure, you do need to water, fertilize, and deadhead from time to time, but you have four times a year to get all revved up about planting!

It's very important to give your container combination a good watering as soon as you're finished planting. This means drenching the soil until you see water draining out the bottom of the container.

Watering

We can't stress enough how important regular watering is! Although larger vessels take longer to dry out than smaller ones do, any container planting is going to dry out much more quickly than plantings in the ground. And here's the problem: if you allow your container to dry completely, it can be hard to remoisten the soil (unless you were to stand it in a big vat of water until you were sure all the soil was moist again — completely impractical). Once the soil has gone bone dry, chances are your plants have gone without water for too long and have begun to go into decline. As mentioned earlier, whereas perennials, trees, and shrubs are tolerant of watering variations in the long run; if they get to the wilting point, they can also have a harder time recovering.

Unfortunately, there is no precise formula for how often a container will need to be watered. How much and how often to water will depend on the kind of plant, the type of potting soil you've selected, the type and size of container, and the weather. Here are a few guidelines:

• Check to see if your container needs watering by sticking in your finger up to the first knuckle (about an inch deep); if the soil feels dry, it needs another watering.

• The kind of plant dictates how much water is needed. Plants that have succulent leaves (sedums and sempervivums) and those with gray or silvery leaves tend to need less water. Those with wide, thin leaves or many leaflets, such as hosta and astilbe, often need more water. Try to use plants that have similar water needs within a given container.

• The kind of container will determine how much you need to water; compositions planted in terra-cotta and concrete need more frequent watering than do those in metal, composites, or glazed ceramics.

• Containers that are exposed to lots of sun and wind will dry out much more quickly than those that aren't. Also, clustering container plantings helps slow down moisture loss, because some plants shade others and because the overall ambient humidity increases.

Take care when watering, and take your time. A quick blast of water can shift plants, disturb the soil cover, and compact the soil around the plants. A slow, gentle, and thorough watering is best — kind of like a light rain that lasts all afternoon. Rainfall is not always dependable, though, so we find the ideal method is to mimic it by using a fine mist or spray for a longer period of time. Water until it runs freely out the bottom of the container.

With a watering can. If you don't have many containers to tend to, watering by hand is manageable. And not only is it manageable, but it's also one of the most satisfying and Zen parts of gardening. This type of watering means that you get up close and personal with your container on a regular basis. You'll also be able to keep an eye out for any pests or diseases and deal with them before they cause problems. Finally, you end up using less water, because you will quickly learn how many watering cans you will need per container and not have a hose running a minute too long, wasting water all the while. Watering with a watering can is still our favorite way to water, hands down.

A good hose and a well-made watering wand are worth investing in.

By hose and wand. This is a better way to go if you have a lot of containers to water. All wands — which we highly recommend over a spray gun or nozzle — come with a valve that you can adjust to set the speed and strength with which the water comes out. You can set it to the loveliest soft flow. But you also have to drag that hose around, risking damaging plants at the edge of a bed or knocking over smaller pots.

Start Watering from Day One

The most important thing to do after planting your container is to water it right away. Watering directly after planting helps to ensure that any air pockets created while planting are closed up, and it just makes sure that the newly planted (and inevitably stressed) plant has access to water immediately, which will help it get back into top shape faster. Thoroughly soak the planting until the water runs out the bottom, which will foster good deep roots. If the entire containerful of soil is moist, the roots will continue to grow out into the pot. If roots encounter a dry patch, however, they won't expand into that territory of the pot.

After that first planting, be sure to stay on top of your watering the first two weeks after transplanting, especially in the summer. Examine your planting daily until you are acquainted with how often it needs to be watered. The straight and simple way is to water when the surface of the soil begins to feel dry. One way to keep the moisture from evaporating quickly is to keep the surface covered with a mulch like moss or buckwheat hulls. Be sure to watch how long it takes your vessel to drain; if the water comes out slowly (or not at all), the drainage holes may need to be unblocked. You don't want to end up with a bog!

The best time of day to do your watering is in the early morning. When you water in the cool of the morning — particularly in the summer — the roots have a chance to soak up the maximum amount of water before it begins to evaporate. When plants start their day with their cells full and fat with water and combine it with plentiful light and sun later on . . . magic! Well, science actually, but it sure does make for happier plants. But sometimes life gets in the way, and if you can't water in the morning, then the evening is the second best. Second best, because having a container full of damp leaves and flowers through the night sets up the perfect condition for diseases such as powdery mildew. When you water in the evening, then, do your best to water only the soil and try not to get the leaves drenched. Watering in the middle of the day is the worst option, because the water tends to evaporate very quickly.

Deadheading

Deadheading is essentially the removal of dead flowers. With many plants, particularly annuals and perennials, deadheading is an easy and satisfying way to keep plants healthy and blooming for the longest period possible. Truth be told, it will keep a perennial, tree, or shrub blooming for only a bit longer, although with annuals, it can extend their flowering lives quite a bit. With most perennials, you will be doing slightly

Sara is trimming off spent blooms from this heuchera before it goes into our magnolia container. Might as well show off that gorgeous foliage!

are starting to get a bit wild and woolly but you're not ready for the next change-out, you can give the perennials growing as the underplantings a more aggressive cut and use the harvest for a bouquet on your desk, beside the sink, by the bedside, or for a friend.

Fertilizing

In addition to frequent watering and a spot in the sun, plants need nutrients to thrive. The three most important nutrients are nitrogen (N), phosphorus (P), and potassium (K). They're listed on the packaging of fertilizer products in that order, represented in a numerical ratio (as in 10-5-10) that describes the percentage in which they are found per weight in the fertilizer. They all are important in the overall health and well-being of plants, but each also plays a specific role. Nitrogen is important to the growth of foliage; phosphorus is key to a plant developing strong roots and flowers; potassium is most important for plants that bear fruit (although all plants need it). Almost all plants grown in a nursery

more than just pinching off a bloom — it often involves cutting a dead flower right down to its stalk. Indeed, with trees and shrubs, you will be deadheading the blooms (using your fingers to pinch off the dead blooms) but mostly to keep the plant looking good and encouraging it to set about growing more woody growth and setting more buds for next year.

Deadheading takes only a minute or so. If your containers

This small evergreen has a healthy root system. Notice the tiny green balls of slow-release fertilizer the nursery added to the soil, making it unnecessary to add more at potting-up time.

setting are grown using significant amounts of fertilizer. This is particularly true of annuals, whose lush flowers and foliage are their prime selling points and tough to create without fertilizer. Perennials, shrubs, and trees don't seem to need as much fertilizer and in fact will often put on weak, leggy growth if too much is applied.

When we're planting perennials, shrubs, and trees in containers, neither of us uses fertilizer very often. We find that given the use of them in the commercial growing process, there tends to be enough residual fertilizer in the potting medium the plants come with. And, of course, when you swap each new season's worth of plants into the container, you'll be adding new soil, which will include some level of organic matter and most likely a nice little boost of fertility.

Despite our tendency to stay away from fertilizers, there are times that warrant their use, such as when you are bringing a good number of transplants from your garden into your container or if you are using the container as a place to beef up a few things before planting them out. When growing or using annuals, you often need to keep fertilizing right through the growing season to keep them flowering and thriving. If and when you fertilize, try to use organic options; we find them to work as well as or better than the chemical ones (for our needs), and the companies that make them tend to be gentler on the earth. See Resources, page 258, for organic-product suggestions.

PRUNING FOR LONG-TERM CARE

Even if you plan on keeping your woody plant in the container for only a couple of seasons, you'll want to prune it occasionally, to encourage good form and to keep the plant healthy. This means pruning away branches that cross each other, as well as those that are unhealthy, weak, damaged, or just plain dead. It also means pruning the roots of the plant, to encourage new growth and ward off root rot.

Snipping Up Top

There are a couple of good guidelines to follow when you're embarking on your pruning adventure, and the first is to determine the right season for pruning the plant you've got. Some trees and shrubs flower on the previous season's growth (spring bloomers); some bloom on the current season's growth (summer bloomers). You don't want to cut off the buds right before they're about to bloom. With woody plants, as a general rule:

• Prune spring-flowering woodies right after they bloom.

Starting Off Right

WE LOVED THIS LITTLE AZALEA at the nursery because of its small size and crisp white blooms. It was a bit leggy in spots for our container, so we knew we had to trim it for a cleaner, more compact look (though its long branches would have been fine in the garden). Sara carefully trimmed back the long branches to an incon-spicuous joint where branches met — often cutting branches back to the center of the plant for a more natural look. If you simply shear the plant at a uniform level, you'll end up with a very unnatural-looking specimen that sticks out like a sore thumb.

• Prune summer-flowering woodies in late winter or early spring.

• Prune evergreens and plants without ornamental flowers in early spring.

Pruning for airflow, size, and shape can be tricky even for experienced gardeners. After all, this kind of pruning is an art; it takes practice to learn to do it well. If you're just starting out, be patient, take your time, and go slow. And remember:

Pruning in early spring has the added benefit that it's much easier to see the woody structure when there are no leaves on the plant!

Just how much can you prune away? Well, for example, when we're dealing with a twiggy, multistemmed shrub like fothergilla, we start by taking out a quarter to a third of the branches from the very base of the plant. This will help ensure good airflow and enough space

for light to get into the center of the shrub —promoting growth and bud set while discouraging disease. You can also use this technique to keep the shrub to a smaller size if you plan to keep it in a container indefinitely.

Begin by taking out the branches or stems that are tallest. This helps to keep the plant compact, but without giving it the shorn effect that can happen if you clip just the branch tips. Once you've done that, stand

Our Favorite Tools

SARA: Snippers of all sizes, hori-hori, Superthrive, watering can (Ro's old oil filling can is the best, just the right hook in the neck), thin nitrile gloves, CobraHead hoe.

RO: Sara has converted me to the ways of the hori-hori. In an ideal world, I would love to wear gloves but I just don't have the dexterity I need, so I don't. I still try from time and time and am still looking for a pair that works for me! Woodpecker shears, a bow saw (though I should admit that I once used it to cut away the bottom third of a frozen pot-bound boxwood. Miraculously it survived and flourished). Whisk broom for dusting soil off a vessel, twine (pretty fun colored is always best).

back and have a look. Often this is will be sufficient pruning, but leave it and come back in the next few days to see if it looks like it needs more. It's always good to be conservative on the first go-round, and to stand back often to examine your handiwork.

If you're planning on keeping a tree or shrub in a container indefinitely, you'll need to regularly prune the plant, starting with its first season in the container following the basic rules above. That being said, it's best if you start by choosing a plant that's not expected to be a giant at maturity. You really don't want to be pruning a tree that will be 30 feet at maturity to fit into a 24-inch-diameter container — it will always be a struggle, both for you and for the health and beauty of the plant.

Root Pruning and Refreshing

Another important practice to follow when keeping a woody tree or shrub in a container is to examine the roots from time to time and refresh the soil while you're at it. We try to do this at least every three years, if not more frequently. This is best done before the plant has leafed out or after the leaves have fallen off (so early spring and late fall; these times also work for root-pruning evergreens).

Start by digging out some of the soil around the plant, to loosen the root ball and make it easier to pull out. Hold the tree firmly by the trunk (or stems, if it's a shrub), right at the base of the plant where it emerges from the soil. Depending on the size of the tree, shake off and/or "tickle" off as much soil as you can. You can also use a hand cultivator to loosen the soil. The idea is to get off as much of the old soil off as possible without damaging the roots. If any of the roots are discolored, unhealthy looking, or beginning to circle the container, it's time to root-prune. Take a pair of pruners and cut away the sections of root that are circling around, as well as those that look sickly.

After we've gotten rid of much of the old soil and root-pruned as needed, we replant with fresh, fertile potting soil. (Even with plants that stay in

Sara uses a hori-hori (a Japanese farmer's knife) to loosen the roots of this small tree and prepare it for planting.

only for a year or two, we like to top off the container each spring with a layer of compost, often when we're swapping in the new spring planting.) Firm it in and water well. To avoid stressing the plant, it's best to do this kind of work on a cool, overcast day (yet another reason for doing it in spring or fall).

Part 2
TWELVE CONTAINERS THROUGH THE YEAR

AT FIRST GLANCE, it might seem like it would be hard to keep a container full of plants looking fresh and eye-catching through the year. But just think of it as a miniature garden, with perennials and shrubs coming and going in and out of their glory and colorful annuals as accents. Certainly, like any garden, it will have its high and low points, with several peaks throughout the year. But often the quiet times provide the most intimate connection with the plants, as the gardener learns to appreciate each plant's quiet beauty — the fading flower, the fuzzy seed head, the bronzy grass blades — and the subtle changing of the seasons as they come and go.

Roanne highlights the chartreuse branches of the dogwood with golden yellow daffodils and cheery purple pansies.

Colorful Sticks

WHY STICKS? Because we love clean lines. We love when all the trees go bare for the winter, when the branches impose a natural grid on the landscape and offer you a new way to see space. We use sticks a lot — in container plantings and floral arrangements, as well as in the garden. Trees and shrubs with nice lines add just as much to the winter landscape as do evergreens, grasses, and plants with seedpods. They continue to look great in the spring, when delicate blooms, buds, or new leaflets adorn their branches. And whether you've planted the whole shrub in a container or simply added its cut branches, sticks give motion, line, and sometimes needed height to the composition.

Some stick shrubs behave better than others in the container. We find that container-grown shrubs (as opposed to field-grown) work better; they've generally been groomed to look great in a contained setting and their branches are usually growing upright and are relatively compact in height and width.

The most reliable stick shrubs are the yellowtwig and redtwig dogwoods (varieties of *Cornus alba* and *Cornus stolonifera*). They are readily available at your garden center and you can usually find them in a number of colors and sizes. They can tolerate somewhat boggy soil and a variety of sun conditions (though, like most plants, they're happiest when they receive full to part sun and are planted in well-drained soil), and they overwinter well in the vessel.

This kind of dogwood looks best when it's trimmed every other year, which heightens the intensity of the color and allows you to shape the plant. In this container combination, we've actually used the trimmed branches as a design element after we planted out the shrub itself. And here's a fun side note: Many times in the past when we've used redtwig dogwood trimmings to decorate conifer combinations for the winter season, the sticks have rooted and sprouted leaves the following summer. Accidental propagation! Love it.

COLORFUL STICKS
Spring

To us, a New England spring means pillowy patches of moss growing along icy woodland streams, clusters of flowering bulbs in front of stone walls, and swaths of branch tips turning a mahogany tone and swelling up in preparation for bloom. We tried to capture that feeling here. We emphasized the yellowness of the sticks by massing narcissus at the base and gave the planting a more ornamental feel by adding the violets and a medley of herbs.

'Jetfire' narcissus

herbs: thyme, parsley, purple sage, marjoram

'Sorbet Babyface' violet

yellowtwig dogwood

yellowtwig
dogwood

'Sunrise'
coreopsis

'Palace Purple'
heuchera

'Kaleidoscope'
glossy abelia

'Gold Haze'
heather

COLORFUL STICKS
Summer

In summer, the yellowtwig dogwood is fully leafed out. Its beautiful yellow sticks are somewhat concealed at this point, and without an underplanting, the composition would feel visually top-heavy. To offset this, we put in a vibrant underplanting, full of color, motion, and gusto, starring the diva glossy abelia (*Abelia* 'Kaleidoscope'). This shrub packs a punch, providing not only intense color but wonderful movement and weight as well.

We find that it's sometimes best to let one plant dictate the seasonal color story — in this case, we found our palette by extracting tones from the foliage of 'Kaleidoscope'. Plum-purple, yellow, chartreuse, orange . . . they're all here, and when artfully arranged, they keep your eyes moving around the composition.

COLORFUL STICKS
Fall

The year we photographed this container, we had a really wet summer. Our dogwood grew huge, so we decided to cut it back hard — down to the base of the plant — harvest its branches, and plant the shrub itself into a garden among redtwig dogwoods (*Cornus alba*) and yuccas (*Yucca*). We have successfully over-wintered containerized dogwoods for many years in sunny conditions, but this one had begun to dominate the rest of the combination. So, we happily moved forward, our dogwood in the ground, sticks harvested and ready to adorn this season's planting.

'Superba' knotweed

orange garden mum

'Fireworks' goldenrod

'Weston's Lollipop' azalea

yellowtwig dogwood

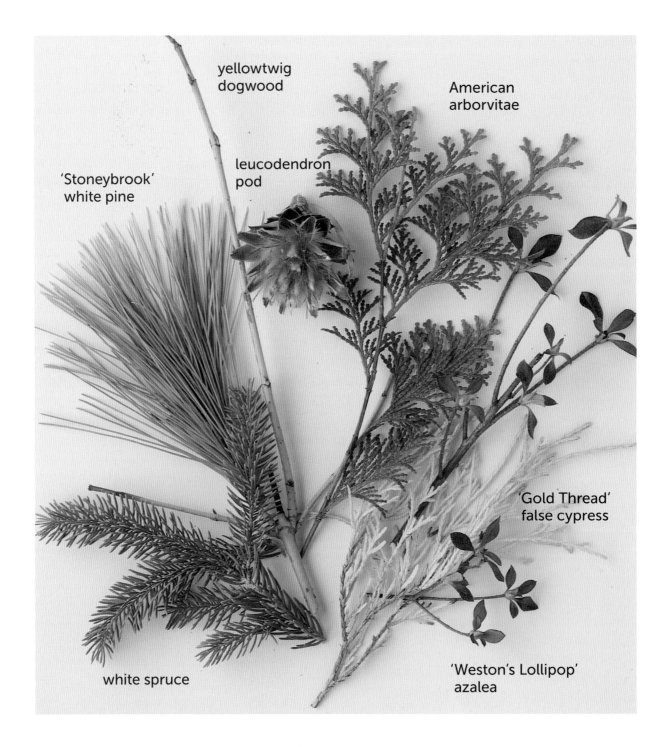

yellowtwig
dogwood

American
arborvitae

'Stoneybrook'
white pine

leucodendron
pod

'Gold Thread'
false cypress

white spruce

'Weston's Lollipop'
azalea

COLORFUL STICKS
Winter

Ro has a soft spot for variegated and yellow-toned conifers; she loves the way they brighten her path on a cold winter or gray spring day. For this planting, we used cuttings from these gorgeous yellow-toned conifers, taken from Ro's gardens. We used 'Stoneybrook' white pine (*Pinus densiflora* 'Stoneybrook') and false cypress (*Chamaecyparis* 'Gold Thread'). There is usually a large selection of these kinds of conifers at most nurseries, so they're quite easy to find. Also, because they're often sold in 1-gallon pots, they're the perfect size to plant in a large container.

For this container planting, by the time winter rolled around, we wanted to continue the cheerful yellow vibe we'd been pushing all year, so these conifer cuttings were perfect. If you've decided to plant out your dogwood, use its cut sticks to complete the look in the container and carry on the "stick" theme. Fill in any negative space between the azalea branches with some cut greens. In addition to the variegated conifer cuttings, we put in some white spruce limbs (left over from the bottom of the Christmas tree) and some American arborvitae (*Thuja occidentalis*). We dressed our planting with native moss and some funky leucodendron pods; you can do the same, or experiment with different kinds of mulch, lichens, or even a bed of pinecones and pine needles.

COLORFUL STICKS
PLANT PALETTES

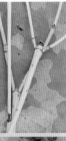

Spring

New Plantings

» 'Jetfire' narcissus
Narcissus 'Jetfire'

WHAT IT IS: bulb
ZONES: 3–7
SWAP OUT: summer

This jaunty, bright yellow-and-orange daffodil arrives with such cheery color in the early season that you can't help but smile when you see it. Its petals are an egg-yolk yellow and the cup is an extraordinary reddish orange. This cultivar is a nice compact size, up to 14 inches tall, and in our composition it's the perfect complement to the yellow twigs of the dogwood.

INTO THE GARDEN: At the end of spring, we pulled these out of the container and found a happy, sunny place in the garden for them. The landscape that surrounds this container is filled with daffodils, so they fit right in. We don't generally add fertilizer to bulbs when we plant them, but as long as you don't overdo it, it won't hurt.

ALTERNATIVES: Other daffodil (*Narcissus*) varieties, such as 'Maria', 'Itzim', 'Jumblie', 'Bantam', and 'Serola'

» 'Sorbet Babyface' violet
Viola 'Sorbet Babyface'

WHAT IT IS: annual
ZONES: n/a
SWAP OUT: summer

The darling little face of this purple-and-white violet is just right for adding the perfect touch of sweetness to this composition. At 3 to 4 inches high, it forms a nice little ring around the taller components of this container. And it is a perfect mixer, diplomatically squeezing in with low herbs.

INTO THE GARDEN: We took out the viola after summer arrived. If the beginning of summer stays cool, the violas could be moved out into little terra-cotta pots of their own or massed in one large shallow bowl until the heat turns them leggy. Continue deadheading until it's time to add them to the compost pile.

ALTERNATIVES: Pansies, perennial violets such as *Viola sororia*, edging lobelia (*Lobelia erinus*), prostrate speedwell (*Veronica* 'Trehane'), periwinkle (*Vinca minor*)

» Herbs: Thyme, parsley, purple sage, marjoram
Thymus, Petroselinum crispum, Salvia officinalis, Origanum majorana

WHAT IT IS: Perennial and annual
ZONES: Sage and thyme (perennials) are hardy to Zone 5
SWAP OUT: summer

We love herbs and find that they are the perfect addition to many containers. They're subtle but beautiful in leaf color and texture. We like thyme for its tiny, almost fuzzy leaves. Curly parsley has bright green leaves and a crisp texture. Purple sage (one of our all-time favorites for mixed container plantings) has elongated oval leaves like cats' tongues, as well as a purple hue that seems to look good with just about any other plant. Marjoram adds a soft leaf with a pleasant oregano scent. All are short enough in stature not to interfere with or take away from the more eye-popping components of this planting. In the summer, they'll come out and be dried to later sprinkle over tofu, grilled squash, or grilled veggie pizza.

ALTERNATIVES: Irish moss (*Sagina subulata*), Scotch moss (*Selaginella kraussiana* 'Brownii'), and other cold-tolerant, steppable ground covers

Yellowtwig dogwood

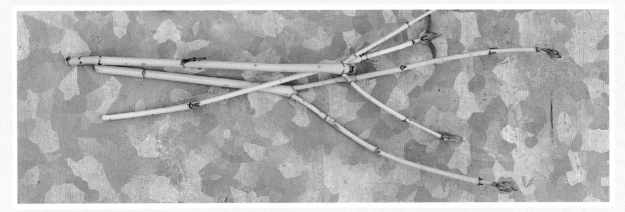

GROW YELLOWTWIG DOGWOOD shrubs in full sun for the brightest bark coloration. The plant will tolerate partial shade, but reduced sun exposure will dull the color display in time. The blooms and berries of yellowtwig dogwood (*Cornus alba* 'Bud's Yellow') are cute but on the whole are not the main feature of this plant.

At the nursery, look for a plant that has a great shape, one whose branches do not cross and whose base looks sturdy and free of damage. Yellowtwig dogwood can grow 6 inches or more in its first year, so keep that in mind. We like to start with a specimen that has been grown in a 3- to 5-gallon pot. Try to find one whose branches look natural, without the buzz-haircut appearance of a plant that's just been pruned back hard. If buzzed is all you can find at your garden center, however, stop by your local florist to see if you can find some cut branches. Add them to your planting to create a more natural look.

Zones: 3–8

Site analysis: The gardener at the property where this container lives had just put in a new mixed border, of which one central element was a sinuous line of golden variegated yuccas (*Yucca* 'Color Guard'). In another nearby border, she has a dense planting of redtwig dogwood, so we wanted to experiment with yellowtwig in our container as an accent to the new color story being told in the garden by the yucca.

Best containers: Pressed concrete or square zinc

Our container choice: For this combination, we chose an antique oil vessel for its relaxed feel. We liked how the branches played off the corrugation that rounds the vessel. The patina gives a nice maturity to the vessel and contrasts well with the backdrop of the newly shingled post-and-beam outbuilding. Remember: If you're planting into an antique-store find like this one (or even just a replica), you'll need to drill drainage holes into it (see page 39). Also, avoid setting metal containers like this one directly on concrete, as they may stain it.

Alternative plants: *Cornus sericea* 'Cardinal', yellowtwig dogwood (*Cornus stolonifera* 'Flaviramea' or 'Silver and Gold'), Japanese maple (*Acer palmatum* 'Sango-kaku'), corkscrew hazel (*Corylus avellana* 'Contorta'), black pussy willow (*Salix gracilistyla* 'Melanostachys')

COLORFUL STICKS
PLANT PALETTES

Summer

New Plantings

» 'Kaleidoscope' glossy abelia

Abelia 'Kaleidoscope'

WHAT IT IS: shrub
ZONES: hardy to Zone 6 (and evergreen in Zone 7)
SWAP OUT: end of summer

Abelia has a lot going on for a little shrub. In spring, chartreuse leaves rimmed in gold appear on its bright red stems. As the summer heat arrives, the golden-colored variegation takes on a creamier appearance. When summer nights begin to cool off, the foliage takes on intense fire tones, from true reds to orange to creamy orange. It's almost tropical looking!

As the fall continues, the plant gradually turns more and more crimson in color. In warmer regions, the foliage will hang on through the beginning of winter, but here in coastal Rhode Island, the leaves are gone by Thanksgiving. This variety is a profuse bloomer —

light pink buds and sweet white flowers appear spring through summer, with final blooms tapering off during autumn.

INTO THE GARDEN: This shrub is a great container choice, as it can stay in the pot from spring to summer and with a heavy mulch can even overwinter there. If you choose to plant it into the garden, select a spot with full to partial sun, which will keep the coloration brilliant. Trim the plant in spring or summer to keep its compact shape, and prune out any water sprouts or other stray branches that appear. Be sure to plant 'Kaleidoscope' somewhere where you can appreciate the early-spring contrast of brilliant red stems and limey yellow new growth. The butterflies enjoy this plant as much as you will!

ALTERNATIVES: Boxleaf honeysuckle (*Lonicera nitida* 'Baggeson's Gold' or 'Lemon Beauty'), euphorbia (*Euphorbia griffithii* 'Fireglow'), spirea (*Spiraea* 'Magic Carpet')

» 'Sunrise' coreopsis

Coreopsis 'Sunrise'

WHAT IT IS: perennial
ZONES: 4–9
SWAP OUT: fall

Reliable, long-blooming, daisy-like flowers arrive in early summer and linger into fall. In the garden, this coreopsis will naturalize effortlessly and will attract butterflies and finches. In the container, its cheery yellow-orange, semi-double blooms bring a wave of color to the underplanting. They mix in nicely among the dogwood stems, adding a middle layer that softens the base of the dogwood and accents the vibrant colors of the glossy abelia. Heat-tolerant and easy to grow, trim it after the first round of blooms in early summer to encourage a fall show.

INTO THE GARDEN: Transplant into the garden in fall in a hot, dry spot. Deadheading extends the bloom, so feel free to cut a few stems while you're out in the garden. Don't cut down the plant for the winter; if you leave the new fall growth at the base, it will offer additional protection and will help ensure successful overwintering. As the plant matures, you can divide it and transition it back into future container combinations. 'Sunrise' is a great mid-height perennial, growing to about 20 inches. Plant it with ornamental grasses, with some low-growing annual verbena dodging in and out of its foliage.

ALTERNATIVES: Coneflower (*Echinacea* 'Sunrise'), blanketflower (*Gaillardia* 'Fanfare'), zinnia (*Zinnia* 'Zowie Yellow Flame'), butterfly weed (*Asclepias* 'Hello Yellow'), marguerite (*Argeranthemum frutescens* 'E. C. Buxton')

» 'Gold Haze' heather
Calluna 'Gold Haze'
WHAT IT IS: perennial
ZONES: 4–7
SWAP OUT: fall

'Gold Haze' has beautiful pale yellow foliage that grows in a nice compact, upright form. White flowers cover the plant from August to October. Be sure the container gets some sun or the foliage will take on a green tinge. Heathers prefer well-drained, humus-rich soil.

INTO THE GARDEN: Come fall, plant into the garden and experiment more with heathers. They offer so much diversity and visually blend into a variety of settings. Heathers bloom year-round in a vast range of colors: white, pale pink, lilac, crimson, and purple. Their tiny florets can appear on yellow, orange, red, gold, gray, or green foliage. Most heathers are evergreen and some even turn a true crimson for the winter. Heathers are happiest in a south-facing garden. Plant them deeply, so the bottommost foliage is resting on the soil, and mulch in with a nice buckwheat mulch.

ALTERNATIVES: Other heathers like *Calluna* 'Red Haze', 'Orange Queen', and 'Blazeaway'; Boston fern (*Nephrolepsis exaltata*); and *Selaginella martensii*

» 'Palace Purple' heuchera
Heuchera 'Palace Purple '
WHAT IT IS: perennial
ZONES: 4–9
SWAP OUT: fall

'Palace Purple' was the first of many purple-leaved heucheras to be introduced into the nurs-

ery trade. There are many more now, some that are darker, some that even have fanciful silver swirls. 'Palace Purple' is widely available and should be on your go-to plant roster. This heuchera's tidy mound of dark, maple-shaped foliage can be employed anywhere you're looking for a reliable punch of color. In the garden, we welcome the small, creamy-white flower spikes that appear in early summer, but this isn't always the case when we use heucheras as container underplantings. Their frothy floral display can be distracting when they're trying to poke through a nice tailored boxwood topiary. Don't be afraid to remove any unwanted blooms for the sake of the overall composition.

INTO THE GARDEN: When grown in full sun, heucheras need even moisture. Deadhead frequently to encourage continued blooming (if that's what you're after). Heucheras have shallow roots, so apply a winter mulch of pine needles after the ground freezes. This will keep the plant insulated and will help prevent root heaving.

COLORFUL STICKS
PLANT PALETTES

ALTERNATIVES: Bugleweed (*Ajuga*) works as a nice alternative to heucheras and should also be a part of your underplanting pantry for "go-to" situations. Euphorbia (*Euphorbia dulcis* 'Chameleon') and some dark-toned sedums (*Sedum*) are other options.

Fall

New Plantings

» 'Weston's Lollipop' azalea
Rhododendron 'Weston's Lollipop'
WHAT IT IS: shrub
ZONES: 4–9
SWAP OUT: spring

The texture and color of 'Weston's Lollipop' in the fall is really a sight to be seen. Blood orange and red-brown foliage appear as teardrop-shaped leaves. This plant has a lot to offer — a beautiful fragrant show of bubblegum pink flowers, a unique patchwork of fall color, and a truly fantastic shape. 'Weston's Lollipop' grows

about 5 feet wide and stays 3 feet tall. In the garden it's a great underplanting for larger conifers and flowering trees.

INTO THE GARDEN: Plant somewhere you can appreciate the fragrance as well as the attractive coloration of the blossoms. The bloom display lingers on a lot longer than most late-flowering azaleas, so get ready! Plant in well-drained soil in full sun to partial shade.

ALTERNATIVES: Daphne (*Daphne* 'Lawrence Crocker'), golden barberry (*Berberis thunbergii* 'Golden Divine'), dwarf sweetspire (*Itea virginica* 'Little Henry'), summersweet (*Clethra alnifolia* 'Ruby Spice')

» Orange garden mum
Chrysanthemum × *grandiflorum*
WHAT IT IS: perennial, often sold as an annual
ZONES: 5–9
SWAP OUT: winter

The mum rounds out the back of the planting, keeping the base lush and full. Its dense, moundy shape works well with the more airy-feeling azalea. We've enjoyed having bright oranges and yellows in this planting and thought the

orange carpet of flowers could give the container a little lift.

INTO THE GARDEN: We composted it when it finished blooming, but you could always try moving it out to a sunny, well-drained spot in the garden.

ALTERNATIVES: Any colorful fall-flowering plant would be appropriate. Try harvest-toned annuals like violets (*Viola*) and African daisy (*Osteospermum*), or bronzy New York aster (*Aster novi-belgii*).

» 'Fireworks' goldenrod
Solidago rugosa 'Fireworks'
WHAT IT IS: perennial
ZONES: 3–9
SWAP OUT: winter

When planted in large clusters, this goldenrod really does look like fireworks. Its tall, arching rays of yellow flowers sparkle above tidy clumps of leaves. Goldenrod has had the misfortune of being deemed the cause of hay fever, which is a misapprehension we should all correct. Plant 'Fireworks' in sun to part shade, and give it a good haircut in June (cut back by about half) to keep it trim and tidy.

INTO THE GARDEN: Plant into a meadow garden in moist,

well-drained soil. It will grow 3 to 4 feet tall by 2 to 3 feet wide. Its display is truly spectacular and looks great when paired with ornamental grasses or with other autumn bloomers such as purple aster (*Aster novi-belgii*) and tall verbena (*Verbena bonariensis*).

ALTERNATIVES: For yellow alternatives, try sneezeweed (*Helenium* 'Butterpat') or sunflower (*Helianthus multiflorus* 'Flore Pleno'). Boltonia (*Boltonia*) is a nice white alternative.

» 'Superba' knotweed
Persicaria affinis 'Superba'

WHAT IT IS: perennial
ZONES: 3–9
SWAP OUT: winter

This dwarf variety makes a wonderful ground cover for the garden, offering three seasons of interest. It starts out purple and gradually changes to a nice glossy green. Pinkish white bottlebrush flowers appear throughout summer and turn deeper pink as the flowers age,

until the foliage is transformed into a wash of true red. Its color holds up in the cold — even after we dug it out of the snow on a chilly October morning in New Hampshire, it still looked remarkable.

INTO THE GARDEN: For best color, plant in full sun. Let it fill in the gaps of the garden or edge the driveway. Its lavender-looking blossoms are very welcoming.

ALTERNATIVES: Heavenly bamboo (*Nandina domestica* 'Technicolor'), chameleon plant (*Houttuynia cordata* 'Chameleon')

Winter

Holdover from Fall

» 'Weston's Lollipop' azalea
Rhododendron 'Weston's Lollipop'

We left 'Lollipop' in the container through the winter, because we liked the grid-like web of branches, with its espresso-toned leaves dangling at the tips. Spring will be a great

time to transplant this azalea to its permanent residence — a mixed shrub border dotted with yellowtwig dogwood, yellow-toned conifers, and other textural plants we experimented with this year in the underplanting of our container.

ALTERNATIVES FOR WINTER: Skimmia (*Skimmia japonica* 'Rubella'), Japanese holly (*Ilex crenata* 'Golden Gem'), American arborvitae (*Thuja occidentalis* 'Golden Tuffet')

ADORNMENTS: Cut yellowtwig sticks; clippings of 'Stoneybrook' white pine (*Pinus strobus* 'Stoneybrook'), false cypress (*Chamaecyparis* 'Gold Thread'), and American arborvitae (*Thuja occidentalis*); two boughs of white spruce; native moss; and leucodendron pods (*Leucodendron rubrum*).

Cool Bark

BECAUSE OF THEIR obsession with flowers, many people overlook the other positive attributes of plants: colorful, textural foliage; charming habit; and, one of our favorites, interesting bark. There are so many woody plants with beautiful, texturally rich bark, whether it's the softly peeling bark of the birch (*Betula*) that reveals a soothing mix of beige, cream, and the palest of pink, or the shining, coppery-smooth surface of a birchbark cherry (*Prunus serrula*), or the shaggy beige strips hanging off the trunk of the seven-son flower (*Heptacodium miconoides*). All of these different trees, with their exquisite bark, bring a whole new visual element to the garden. We are also drawn to trees with stellar bark because it helps to accentuate the linear nature of a tree, particularly when it is leafless in the winter and early spring. Even a small tree's striking lines add an element of height to a space; a tree that has unusual bark will have more of an impact in a narrow or low space, even in the deep of winter.

The color of the bark, persisting as it does throughout the year, can provide an unusual jumping-off point in the design of a container. We chose to use river birch (*Betula nigra* 'Little King') to highlight this attribute. Birch is a familiar plant to those of us who grew up on or near the eastern shores of North America. White birches are often found growing in large groves, making the forest appear as a white-and-black-flecked wall. The curls of bark hang off the tree at all times of the year as the trees constantly but slowly shed their outer layers. Depending on the container and plant companions you choose for it, birch can evoke anything from a rustic, woodsy feel to a sleek, urban sensibility. In containers, white birch trunks create a mini-island of calm and provide interest all season long. We also like to use cut birch branches in the garden or even just placed in a bundle near the front door, adding a touch of woodland to any setting through the winter.

COOL BARK
Spring

We wanted this contained corner of spring to liven up our muted backdrop. But we didn't want to go so crazy that it felt jarring, because we still wanted the planting to have a woodsy, cozy feeling. The daffodils provide height to help connect the underplanting to the birch trunk and branches. The middle of the planting — near the trunk of the tree — is open and we can't plant deeply there, so we stripped the soil from the bulbs when we unpotted them, nestling them directly on top of the birch's root ball and covering them with a handful of soil. The catmint provides a nice moundy shape, and its soft silvery cast picks up the silver-pink tones of the tree bark. The trailing green leaves of bearberry (*Arctostaphylos uva-ursi*) and periwinkle (*Vinca minor*) soften the hard edges of the pot.

'Thalia' daffodil

periwinkle

river birch

'Massachusetts' bearberry

Labrador violet

'Little Titch' catmint

river birch

'Burgundy Lace'
lady fern

'Massachusetts'
bearberry

'Caitlin's Giant'
bugleweed

'Burgundy Glow'
bugleweed

periwinkle

mukdenia

COOL BARK
Summer

It was important to us to keep the purple and silver tones with which we started this composition. We just decided to deepen them in the summer palette to richer tones of purple, burgundy, and near black. The Labrador violet (*Viola labradorica*) was growing profusely, its dark plum leaves nestling against the birch nicely. We also wanted something dark and crunchy; something that could ground the planting and serve as a visual opposite from the lacy, ghostlike greens, silvers, and plums of the burgundy lace fern. Bugleweed's rippling, near-black leaves made a perfect contrasting element. The mukdenia (*Mukdenia rossii*) was added to bring another foliage shape into the mix. Its cute, fan-like mittens sociably pop in and out of the base of the planting. The vinca and bearberry have become regulars and were too happy for us to take out. They soften the edge and give a clean sparkle to the underplanting.

COOL BARK
Fall

Birch takes on a golden glow in the fall. Yellow, brown, and rust-colored leaves dangle and rattle in the breeze. We wanted to celebrate that coloration by creating a matching palette — one that captures the fall display that appears along the river's edge. During a fall container junket, we were sitting by the river, coffee in hand, admiring the native landscape. We spoke of our favorite garden designers — those who were in tune with nature and emulated that beauty by making it more accessible for the viewer. We wanted our containers to capture a little slice of nature and bring it up close. We wanted our planting to feel like a big swatch of honey-toned grasses dancing at the water's edge.

autumn fern

mukdenia

periwinkle

eastern teaberry

pheasant's eye

'Massachusetts' bearberry

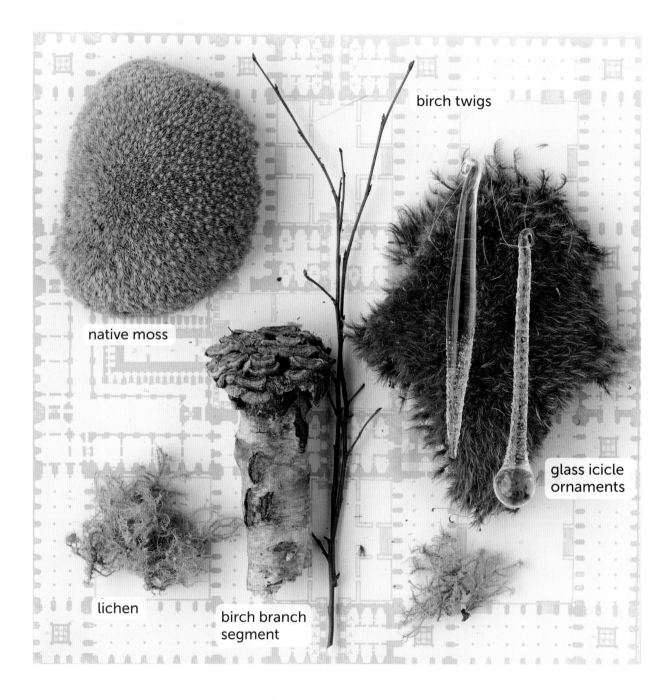

native moss

birch twigs

lichen

birch branch
segment

glass icicle
ornaments

COOL BARK
Winter

To create our magical miniature landscape, we used assorted pinecones, reindeer moss, native mosses, lichens, and hypertufa mushrooms around the base of the tree and hung icicle ornaments from its branches.

As the cool weather settled in, we realized that we wanted our birch to keep that woodland forest feel into the winter months. Nothing looks more like a woodland fairytale backdrop than the snow-filled moonlight glistening off the birch bark! To emphasize this feeling, we hung glass icicle ornaments from the birch branches, swapped out all the underplantings, and arranged a tapestry of mosses, lichens, pinecones, and faux mushrooms.

COOL BARK
PLANT PALETTES

it in check and from looking scraggly. Plant periwinkle out in the garden where you need a quick carpet of dark green.

ALTERNATIVES: Golden creeping jenny (*Lysimachia nummularia* 'Aurea'), variegated strawberry (*Fragaria vesca* 'Variegata'), thyme (*Thymus vulgaris*), wintercreeper (*Euonymus fortunei* 'Kewensis'), spotted geranium (*Geranium maculatum*)

» Labrador violet
Viola labradorica
WHAT IT IS: perennial
ZONES: 3–8
SWAP OUT: summer

This dark beauty likes to spread itself around. The small, romantic purple flowers are perfectly complemented by the leaves, which are almost black. It is happiest in a part-shade, woodland setting but will grow almost anywhere — so keep an eye out for seedlings that pop up. Seedlings can be easily transplanted into small pots or even eggshells.

INTO THE GARDEN: Even after the initial spring flush of blos-

soms, this violet's foliage is so dramatic and pretty that it's a great plant to leave in or move around the pot. If you take it out, it's adaptable and nice to just tuck beneath a shrub as an understory planting.

ALTERNATIVES: Other violets (we love the perennial *Viola* 'Etain' and 'Rebecca', *V. sororia* 'Freckles', and bird's-foot violet [*V. pedata*]), lilyturf (*Ophiopogon planiscapus* 'Nigrescens'), celandine (*Ranunculus ficaria* 'Brazen Hussy'), barrenwort (*Epimedium* × *versicolor* 'Sulphureum'), bugleweed (*Ajuga reptans* 'Caitlin's Giant')

Planting Bulbs into the Garden

MOST PEOPLE ASSOCIATE PLANTING bulbs with fall, yet many bulbs do just as well when planted "in the green," meaning when they have finished blooming but still have their green leaves. The first step is to pull the bulbs gently out of the container. Separate them into individuals and plant each bulb so that it is at a depth that is three times the height of the bulb. For example, if a daffodil bulb is 2 inches tall, the bottom of the bulb should be planted 6 to 7 inches deep. Backfill the hole and water well. The only hazard with planting in the green is that it needs to be done immediately, straight from pot to ground.

» 'Massachusetts' bearberry

Arctostaphylos uva-ursi 'Massachusetts'

WHAT IT IS: shrub
ZONES: 2–6
SWAP OUT: spring

The lustrous evergreen leaves are the highlight of this charming low-growing shrub (we find it to be a friendlier-looking option for cotoneaster; it has a similar bony structure but is softer and more flowing). In spring, small, pinky white flowers appear, followed by red berries in the fall (sometimes they don't show up if the plant is used in a container).

INTO THE GARDEN: This heath-family relative is a bear — in that it can handle a wide range of conditions with ease. In the garden, it prefers quick-draining soil and full sun, but ours was happy all year long in this part-shady, damp situation. When and if you plant it out, try to give it better drainage and more sun than we offered here.

ALTERNATIVES: blueberry (*Vaccinium angustifolium*), cranberry (*Vaccinium macrocarpon*), junipers (*Juniperus*), rockspray cotoneaster

(*Cotoneaster horizontalis*), hemlock (*Tsuga canadensis* 'Cole's Prostrate')

Summer

Holdover from Spring

» 'Massachusetts' bearberry

Arctostaphylos uva-ursi 'Massachusetts'

Bearberry holds its upright, green composure while the heat wears down those around it, so we kept it in the container. No reason to fix it if it ain't broke. But you could move it into a container of its own if you need the container space for another plant. It could be fun to have a little grouping of unexpected small shrubs and such in terracotta on your porch leading into winter — provided they look as smart and stylish as bearberry.

» Periwinkle

Vinca minor

Blooming periodically until the frosts arrive, periwinkle is another doer. It just keeps on keepin' on, draping and lying about in its soft, elegant yet casual way. We left periwinkle

in as summer turned to fall. We liked the dark glossy green of her foliage as a backdrop to the more dramatic yellows in the composition.

New Plantings

» 'Burgundy Lace' lady fern

Athyrium 'Burgundy Lace'

WHAT IT IS: perennial fern
ZONES: 4–8
SWAP OUT: fall

Japanese painted ferns burst onto the garden scene several years ago with the excellent *Athyrium niponicum* var. *pictum*. These ferns became the hottest fern since Victorian times, when ferns were, well, really hot. Now there are a good number of excellent cultivars such as 'Ghost' (which is really a cross between *A. n.* var. *pictum* and *A. filix-femina*), 'Branford Beauty', and 'Lady in Red'. Almost all ferns prefer deep, humusy, moist soil in part or full shade.

INTO THE GARDEN: We pulled this out of the container when we did the changeover to autumn. It would have been happy in the container until the frosts started to set in. Fall is a

COOL BARK
PLANT PALETTES

good time for planting ferns into the garden, when the soil is cool and damp and drought is unlikely. If you happen to have a hot, dry autumn, just keep an eye on your newly planted lovely; it will need a drink or two (or five) if the going gets hot.

ALTERNATIVES: Black brass buttons (*Leptinella squalida*) 'Platt's Black', *Athyrium* 'Ghost' or 'Lady in Red', dusky cranesbill (*Geranium phaem* 'Sambor'), *Geranium* 'Midnight Reiter'

» Bugleweed
Ajuga reptans 'Caitlin's Giant' and 'Burgundy Glow'
WHAT IT IS: perennial ground cover
ZONES: 3–9
SWAP OUT: fall

These creeping ground covers are a good choice for anyone who has a tough, shady place where not much grows. I know, I'm making them sound like bottom-of-the-barrel plants, but they're not. They're just tough and vigorous, needing only average soil and part shade or dappled sun to thrive. Some of the new cultivars are less apt to

elbow out other prized posses- sions, and 'Caitlin's Giant' and 'Burgundy Glow' bring to the table splendid foliage. 'Caitlin's Giant' has larger than usual leaves (up to 6 inches long), but it is the deep burgundy color that has many gardeners won over. 'Burgundy Glow' is a spec- tacular, quasi-kaleidoscope of color: pink, white, and pale green swirling together, with the newer leaves flushing out in an almost hot pink. Both are very attractive and worthy container-garden additions.

INTO THE GARDEN: If it's kept in the container, it'll thrive until the snow really begins to fly — it's that tough. We took out ours and planted it into little clay pots for the fall and then trans- planted it into the garden in late autumn. It is best to site any bugleweed in an area where you can keep an eye on it

ALTERNATIVES: Heuchera (*Heuchera* 'Obsidian'), tricolor sage (*Salvia officinalis* 'Tricolor'), chocolate mint (*Mentha* 'Mint Chocolate')

» Mukdenia
Mukdenia rossii
WHAT IT IS: perennial
ZONES: 6–9
SWAP OUT: winter

We first met this plant when it was enthusiastically offered up to us as a "great woodlander" by our friend and excellent plantsman Ed Bowen. (When Ed offers you a plant, you take it.) The leaves are super glossy, dark green, and shaped sort of like a maple's. They can turn many of the same red, yellow, and orange tones as a maple. If they're particularly comfortable in your garden, they'll send up wands of delicate white flow- ers in the spring. Mukdenia is a member of the saxifrage family — like bergenia — easy to tell by their similar thick, fleshy rhizomes. They spread in a gentle, kind manner. They are happiest in full or part shade in fertile, moist, well-drained soil.

INTO THE GARDEN: We left the mukdenia in the container until the winter planting because it just looked so pretty there among the birch stems and such. And it stayed pleased with itself, turning a bright golden yellow and then fading only a few weeks before the change-up. No red in it at all, not this year. If you want to take out the mukdenia after the summer season, however, plant it right into the garden where you would settle hostas, ferns, bergenias (*Bergenia*), leadwort (*Pulmonaria*), and other shade-loving beauties.

ALTERNATIVES: Bergenia (*Bergenia cordifolia*), sweet woodruff (*Galium odoratum*), wood anemone (*Anemone nemorosa*), globeflower (*Trollius* × *cultorum*), master-wort (*Astrantia major*), bear's breeches (*Acanthus mollis*)

Fall

Holdovers from Summer

» Periwinkle
Vinca minor

Periwinkle provides a glossy green leaf for the eye to rest on and for the shiny scarlet berries of wintergreen to sparkle on.

» Bearberry
Arctostaphylos uva-ursi

The shiny, dark green leaves begin to turn a bronzy-reddish color as Jack Frost settles in for the winter. This is another one of those lovely acid-loving, low-growing shrubs that really aren't that pleased about being moved about, particularly in the cold weather. Either leave it in place until spring and then

take it out with a large amount of soil around it, transplanting it gingerly in sun or part shade; or transplant it into a pot in early winter with as much soil as possible and store it in a cool but frost-free place.

» Mukdenia
Mukdenia rossii

Generally speaking, *Mukdenia rossii* turns red in fall, but ours turned a lovely golden yellow, which suited us fine, as it looked great with the other yellow and gold plants in the composition.

We left it in for the winter, figuring it would be okay spending the cold season in a big concrete container, and that it would prefer not being planted out in the garden in the

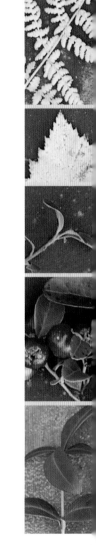

Sunken Pots

NOT SURE WHERE IN THE GARDEN to plant something that's been swapped out of its container? If it's fall, try potting up the transplant, sinking the whole thing (pot and all) into the ground, and mulching well. This way, it'll be easy to find again in spring and super easy to pull up and plant in its final home.

Also, some transplants just survive the winter better this way. Mukdenia, in particular, is one that tends to struggle through the winter if you don't plant it in early fall or spring. Sara has much better luck overwintering plants in pots sunk into the ground, rather than plonking them right into the garden.

COOL BARK
PLANT PALETTES

freezing weather. If you really want it out of your container (*Note:* It will die back to the rhizome anyway, so you won't see it), you could transplant it into a pot (see Sunken Pots, page 89), sink it in the garden, and mulch it.

New Plantings

» Autumn fern
Dryopteris erythrosora
WHAT IT IS: fern
ZONES: 2–6
SWAP OUT: late fall

This lovely fern has somewhat glossy, triangular fronds that are quite colorful in the spring and then ease into a pale green and finally a golden color as they die off with the coming of cool weather. They prefer shade and moist soil with ample organic matter.

INTO THE GARDEN: We chose to take it out in late fall, because we knew we wanted the space for other, more sparkly things. Its golden hue picked up on the many and varied shades of yellow that were present in

this composition in the autumn months.

ALTERNATIVES: Ferns such as *Dryopteris clintonia, D. affinis, D. goldieana,* and *D. marginalis*

» Eastern teaberry
Gaultheria procumbens
WHAT IT IS: shrub
ZONES: 3–6
SWAP OUT: winter

This shrub = holiday season! When the weather starts to cool off, its glossy, dark green leaves turn a burnished red, providing the perfect backdrop to its stunning red berries and sweet little white flowers. This very low-growing (4 to 6 inches tall) shrub is a splendid addition to the fall and winter garden, well, all four seasons really, but especially late in the gardening season. It thrives when grown in acid, moist, humusy soil in the shade or partial shade. When the leaves are crushed, its trademark wintergreen smell is released into the air.

INTO THE GARDEN: We transplanted it into a few pots and stored them in a dark, cool place until spring because transplanting it out in the cold weather is not really ideal; in fact, not even

close to ideal. Little woodland plants like these that hail from scruffy, acid soils tend to be a bit finicky about transplanting. It is best done in the spring or early fall.

ALTERNATIVES: Bunchberry (*Cornus canadensis*), partridgeberry (*Mitchella repens*), plumbago (*Ceratostigma plumbaginoides*)

» Pheasant's eye
Leycesteria formosa 'Golden Lanterns'
WHAT IT IS: shrub
ZONES: 7–9
SWAP OUT: winter

We love the way this small, somewhat delicate shrub looks in this composition. Its fall color is a pale straw yellow with a wash of pale brownish violet. I know, sounds totally gross, but it was perfect. This is a classic case of purchasing something on sharp discount at the nursery, late in the season, without knowing much about it. We divided the shrub into two parts in order to spread it around the composition.

INTO THE GARDEN: Turns out it is a bit on the tender side, even for us in Zone 6–7, so we took it out of the composition for the winter (it didn't add much once the leaves were gone), planted it in a protected part-shade spot, and mulched it heavily.

ALTERNATIVES: Forsythia (*Forsythia* 'Kumon'), *Amsonia hubrectii*, Japanese fountain grass (*Hakonechloa macra* 'Aureola')

Winter

To create our magical miniature landscape, we used assorted pinecones, reindeer moss, native mosses, lichens, and hypertufa mushrooms around the base of the tree, and hung icicle ornaments from its branches.

When decorating your container with these materials, try to keep mosses intact. Moss underplantings look most natural when the shape is irregular. After all, mosses can be found in a variety of shapes and sizes — some look like puffy little clouds, others like sponges, and still others like a roll of carpet. It's a good idea to let the moss take on the shape it would naturally; don't try to flatten out a puffy cloud or puff up a flat carpet. If you run out of moss, that's okay. Fill the gaps with other elements of nature — pine needles, mulch, and leaf mold can tie an underplanting together nicely and will help keep the soil (and thus the plants) more protected from the damaging effects of winter's freezing and thawing cycles.

Cluster pinecones and lichens in groups, looking for natural gulleys in your moss landscape, or use picked pinecones (see page 218) to blend the different mosses together in a visually cohesive way. The picks will also help keep the underplanting intact. If you feel you need further adornments, look for interesting treasures from nature — pods, antlers, unique stones, and stumps can look great nestled among the base of the planting. Add a bit of sparkle to the branches — hang glass icicles or make your own ice creations and adorn the birch's beautiful branches.

Off-Season Blooms

THE SUMMER GARDEN is often focused on perennials and annuals, rich as they are in color and fragrance. However, there is a wide range of shrubs and trees that can light up the garden in the same way, while providing excellent qualities during the rest of the gardening season. Many offer attractive fall foliage, along with colorful berries or textural seedheads.

There are many that flower abundantly in the sun, attracting the buzz and twitter of bees and birds — among them summersweet (*Clethra alnifolia*), bluebeard (*Caryopteris* × *clandonensis*), butterfly bush (*Buddleia davidii*), sweetspire (*Itea virginica*), smokebush (*Cotinus coggygria*), and elderberry (*Sambucus canadensis*). We decided to look for one that would be happy in the quiet, dappled shade of a friend's garden, and chose a summer-flowering azalea (*Rhododendron* 'Weston's Sparkler'). Using this azalea — one of the many incredible crosses that have come from the venerable Weston Nurseries — may be an unusual choice, but we loved the idea of color and fragrance from an unlikely source. Plus, the little specimen was more than content to settle into its container and wait for its high season to arrive, right when and where we needed a bit of sparkle.

Many of the Weston summer-blooming azaleas (most are crosses between native swamp azaleas and sweet azaleas) are well known for their stunning array of colors, bloom time, and fragrance, as well as hardiness and resistance to mildew. (See The Azaleas of Summer, on page 104.) Among the Weston hybrids, there is a tremendous range in colors; we recommend that you buy your azalea when it's in bloom, so you can choose just the right color for your planting.

OFF-SEASON BLOOMS
Spring

This planting was truly as an experiment in combinations. The existing pool that the homeowners had built 10 years before was so elegant, sleek, and simple that it needed no embellishment. Nonetheless, we wanted to try out a few new plant combinations through an entire gardening season, on a small scale, to see what might work in the future. Plus, we wanted to see if the bright pink summer-blooming azalea would look out of place. It didn't. We loved it and the homeowners did, too.

In the spring, we wanted the bergenia and the columbine to be the stars; the oxalis and the brass buttons provide a textural backdrop to the other two plants. This quartet is about texture and foliage, ferny-ness and weighty-ness, light and dark, bold and delicate. We took the opportunity to play with texture and form before the summer (and its flowers) arrived.

'Overture'
bergenia

red columbine

red clover

New Zealand brass
buttons

stinking hellebore

'Weston's Sparkler'
azalea

'Overture' bergenia

fringed
bleeding heart

OFF-SEASON BLOOMS
Summer

This summer design was mostly about the azalea and its bold color and spicy-sweet fragrance. The bleeding heart (*Dicentra*) and the bergenia are just providing a bit of textural interest for when the flowering display goes by. The bleeding heart has motion that spills out of the side of the vessel, softening the hard lines of the container.

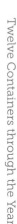

OFF-SEASON BLOOMS
Fall

Here, the focus returns to the bergenia and its super-shiny, smoldering red leaves. They almost glow in this woodland locale. The red is set off by the electric purple of the asters, creating a visual deluxity. Later into the autumn, the leaves of the azalea will begin to turn to an elegant, deep burgundy-red, as though mimicking the bergenia.

'Weston's Sparkler' azalea

'Overture' bergenia

purple aster

cryptomeria

pieris

skimmia (male)

skimmia (female)

boxwood

redtwig dogwood

OFF-SEASON BLOOMS
Winter

Our little azalea is still in good shape in its container overlooking the ice-covered wading pool. We thought it would be fun to over-winter it in the vessel and try it out on the other side of the property next year. Late-blooming azaleas can tolerate more sun and wind than their broadleaf counterparts do, so next year we'll push the limits and place the planting in a more exposed spot. To dress up the container for the holidays, we added some redtwig dogwood branches and a garland of boxwood adorned with other cut greens and berries.

OFF-SEASON BLOOMS
PLANT PALETTES

Spring

New Plantings

» **'Overture' bergenia**
Bergenia cordifolia 'Overture'
WHAT IT IS: perennial
ZONES: (5) 6–9; depends largely
on which cultivar you choose

By far the yummiest part of
this plant is the leaf — crisp,
glossy, bright green, and bold.
Depending on the cultivar, the
leaves are long and strappy
or thick, rounded, and almost
ruffled on the edge. And in
the fall, they turn a burnished
red — delicious!

Bergenias are fairly adaptable
once they get going. Our container planting was surrounded
by "mama" and "baby" bergenias
throughout the surrounding
damp woodland; gardeners we
know who've had them for years
have success with them even
in dry shade. Lovely bright pink
flowers come up in early spring
and continue until at least mid-
spring — a bonus.

INTO THE GARDEN: Bergenias
grow from thick, fleshy

rhizomes, and this is the manner in which they spread to
become big, hefty clumps. If
you want to keep them in the
composition, as we did, just let
them be — the entire planting
likes to be well watered, and the
bergenias take this in stride.
If you want to move them out,
do so with care. Be sure to get
enough rooty bits (you will see
the roots attached to the main
rhizomatous stalk) to allow
them to settle into their new
home, and water them well
through the summer months.

ALTERNATIVES: *Farfugium
japonicum,* hosta (*Hosta siebol-
dii* or *Hosta* 'Drinking Gourd'),
wild ginger (*Asarum canadensis*), *Mukdenia rossii* 'Crimson
Fans', *Ligularia dentata*

» **Red columbine**
Aquilegia canadensis
WHAT IT IS: perennial
ZONES: 4–7
SWAP OUT: summer

This delicate, ferny woodland
delight is a perfect contrast to
the hefty bergenia. Columbines
come in almost all flower colors, and sizes, but we chose
the diminutive (in flower size,
not plant size) native because

it suited the garden around
the container planting, and we
wanted to plant it out afterward.
Next time we might try the
cultivar 'Corbett', which is the
same species but a pale lemon
yellow. Maybe we'd combine it
with azalea 'Weston's Lemon
Drop' with a white bergenia.
But we digress. Columbines
can take dappled or part shade,
though they flower best in full
sun. They're not fussy, and will
grow easily in average, well-
drained soil.

INTO THE GARDEN: Columbine
does nicely as a container
plant and we might have left
it in had we not yet another
cheery little plant with ferny
foliage with which to replace
it. So, we planted it out into the
garden nearby to mingle with
ferns, hellebores, bergenias,
and epimediums. If left in the
container, the columbine would
have kept going with the ferny
foliage until the dreaded, dis-
figuring leaf miner showed up.
This is perhaps another reason
to plant it out. Leaf miner is a
tiny pest that zips around on
the surface of the columbine's
leaf and makes a crazy, maze-
like pattern — it looks as if some

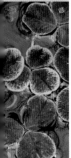

'Weston's Sparkler' azalea

SLOW TO LEAF OUT IN THE SPRING, 'Weston's Sparkler' gives its underplantings and the surrounding garden a chance to shine. When the leaves come out, they are a blue-green shade with a soft pale green underside. Come late June and early July, this happy little azalea lets loose with a bevy of ruffled dark pink flowers and a deliciously spicy-sweet fragrance. The flowering season lasts about two weeks, but the foliage continues in its green softness through the summer and early fall. By late November, the foliage takes on gentle, deep tones of red and burgundy.

We like the compact habit of the azalea and the tight branch structure, which looks great even in spring. The leaves turn a deep hunter green in summer and serve as the perfect backdrop for all the candy-colored blossoms. We chose a pink-flowering azalea but could have just as easily selected a yellow or orange variety. Culturally, these azaleas are suited to the woodland fringe or to the edge of bogs, with full sun or partial shade.

We planted ours in spring and the growth it put on before flowering was impressive to the point that the flowers were partially hidden by it. We did our underplanting for summer and then stood back to see if we wanted to trim it. We waffled, because the new growth gave the composition such a fresh feeling. In the end, we cut back the new growth to show off the blossoms to the best advantage.

Zones: 4–8

Site analysis: We loved this little man-made pool with its crisp lines and smooth, black water softened by a few water lilies (*Nymphaea*) and the odd bullfrog. This water-lily pool sits beside a natural vernal pond, which comes and goes through the gardening season. In the spring, this site is rich with ephemerals as well as the emerging growth of low-growing azaleas, skimmia (*Skimmia*), and hosta (*Hosta*). In summer, the upper woodland canopy closes in, and we felt it could benefit from a bright pink burst of color.

Best containers: We looked for a vessel that would echo the modern lines of the pool. A dark gray concrete bowl or a dark gray or black vase-shaped oval would have worked well.

Our container choice: This black-glazed quasi-cube seems to be the perfect container for this situation. Its color echoes that of the pool directly behind it, and its shape — a blend of the shapes that surround it (part cube, part vase) — brings a nice balance for the size and scale of the azalea.

Alternative plants: Japanese spirea (*Spiraea japonica* 'Goldflame' or 'Ogon'), crape myrtle (*Lagerstroemia indica*), chastetree (*Vitex agnus-castus*), glossy abelia (*Abelia grandiflora*)

OFF-SEASON BLOOMS
PLANT PALETTES

miniature gnome got into his bumper car and went nuts.

ALTERNATIVES: Primrose (*Primula vulgaris*), Lenten rose (*Helleborus orientalis*), bleeding heart (*Dicentra eximia* or *D. formosa*), yellow corydalis (*Corydalis lutea*)

» New Zealand brass buttons
Leptinella squalida 'Platt's Black'
WHAT IT IS: perennial ground cover
ZONES: 6–9
SWAP OUT: summer

A newly popular, mat-forming ground cover, New Zealand brass buttons is a lovely and unusual substitute for moss. Its leaves look very feathery and light; we especially like this darker cultivar because it really is a strange color and gives container plantings a textural boost. Grown best in full sun with moist, rich soil, it is also beautiful in part shade, though it might not flower — which is fine, because the flowers, or brass buttons, are not particularly attractive anyway. I mean, really, where *are* brass buttons attractive other than on a sports coat or a woollen cardigan?

The Azaleas of Summer

THIS FOURTH-GENERATION, family-run nursery in Hopkinton, Massachusetts, is perhaps best known for its introduction of *Rhododendron* 'PJM', the ubiquitous, pinky mauve azalea that is grown everywhere in the New England landscape and beyond. It was the first hybridizing success for Ed Mezzitt, who was beginning to turn his hand to his family's business and, in particular, to the art of hybridizing azaleas; this led to many beautiful plant introductions. He spent a significant amount of time in the 1960s and '70s developing a group of azalea cultivars that bloom late in the season (usually after July 1 in many parts of New England); have fragrant blooms and bright, cheerful colors; and tend to have a wide, upright form. Any and all of them are worth having in the garden, and are lovely in a container. They're happy in full sun to part shade, hardy to Zone 4, and grow best in moist soil.

INTO THE GARDEN: We took it out, dug a shallow little divot, plonked it down, and watered it in. We actually even stepped firmly around the stem to make sure all of the roots were in touch with the soil below. A couple of weeks later, we gave it a drink with a diluted organic fertilizer. Alternatively, it could certainly have stayed in the container with its friends and not minded a bit.

ALTERNATIVES: Irish moss (*Sagina subulata*), club moss (*Selaginella kraussiana*), *Mazus reptans*

» Red clover
Trifolium repens 'Atropurpureum'
WHAT IT IS: perennial
ZONES: 3–11

This plant is clover, yes . . . that very same clover you either love or hate in your yard. There are several quite pretty cultivars on the market, including this fine burgundy one. We love its deep, rich color edged with just a touch of green. It is perfect for winding in and around other big, more muscular plants, softening the edges where needed. It is a low-growing number, not exceeding 10 inches in height, and forms nice clumps when given sun and moist, rich soil.

INTO THE GARDEN: This pretty purple legume has invasiveness in its blood, but we don't find that it ever gets out of hand. We like the way it mingles politely in the garden. We pulled it out and planted it in pots for putting here and there in the house, and then finally planted it out when it started getting leggy from lack of sun. You could keep it in the container outdoors as long as it doesn't get too lanky due to a part-shade location. This is an example of using a plant we love but the plant not loving the location — at least not for too long.

ALTERNATIVES: *Trifolium* 'Dragon's Blood', bugleweed (*Ajuga reptans* 'Burgundy Glow' or 'Caitlin's Giant'), maidenhair vine (*Muehlenbeckia complexa*)

Summer

Holdover from Spring

» 'Overture' bergenia
Bergenia cordifolia 'Overture'
The bergenia stays crisp and green, playing the perfect supporting role to the sparklers above it.

New Plantings

» Fringed bleeding heart
Dicentra eximia
WHAT IT IS: perennial
ZONES: 3–7
SWAP OUT: fall

This pretty, petite shade-lover is the perfect follow-up to the ferny foliage of the columbine (*Aquilegia*). Even more divided, its foliage is a nice complement to the smaller, more slender pink or white bleeding heart flowers that dangle from the stems. Don't let your guard down, however; despite appearances it is very tough and very prolific in seeding around. This small bleeding heart will wend its way into your heart and then into your shade garden with ease. Take care to pull up seedlings where you find them in unwelcome locations.

INTO THE GARDEN: Initially, we dug up ours from the surrounding garden, so after spending the summer in the container, we put it back into the garden without more than a good watering in. It could be left in the container, but bleeding hearts, big and small, tend to wilt away when the hot dry days

OFF-SEASON BLOOMS
PLANT PALETTES

of late summer and fall come along. You could pop in a frilly little annual fern to fill the gap between late summer and the autumn changeout.

ALTERNATIVES: Maidenhair fern (*Adiantum pedantum*), *Corydalis solida* 'Beth Evans', *Corydalis lutea*, columbine (*Aquilegia* spp.), rue (*Ruta graveolens*)

» Stinking hellebore
Helleborus foetidus
WHAT IT IS: perennial
ZONES: 6–9
SWAP OUT: fall

An excellent addition to the helleboriphile's garden, the stinking hellebore has tall stalks that hold up to 40 green flowers per stem in mid-spring, but it is the slightly toothed palmshaped leaves that make it a plant worth keeping through the year. It's happy in part shade with a nice, humus-y soil but can grow well in dry shade if given sufficient water when first

planted. If you can find *H. foetidus* 'Red Silver', it is a striking version of this plant with silver-gray leaf markings and red stems.

INTO THE GARDEN: Once the spring season is over, plant the hellebores into the garden. They require part shade and moist but well-drained soil to start. Once they become established (after having grown in your garden for a couple of years), they will need less water.

ALTERNATIVES: Christmas rose (*Helleborus niger*) or Lenten rose (*Helleborus orientalis*)

Amped-Up Asters

IN THE PAST FEW YEARS, nurseries have started selling little perennial asters for fall displays. Technically, these asters are perennials, but they've been so pinched back, fertilized, and otherwise prodded to produce a ton of blooms on a little plant that they act more like annuals. They look fantastic, of course, but their true nature is to be bigger, lankier, and not quite as floriferous as the amped-up plants at the nursery. So, while these particular asters are great for fall color and are worth planting into the garden afterward, they won't stay as they've been grown the first year. Frankly, unless they're coddled, they may not come back after being planted into the garden because of the stress they experienced in that first year.

Fall

Holdovers from Summer

» **'Overture' bergenia**
Bergenia cordifolia 'Overture'

Its glossy leaves turn a rich crimson red and stay that way for months. Hope for a snowless December so that you can enjoy them all the way through until the New Year. Alternatively, you can swap it out for bok choy and other fun Asian veggies, or skip the crunchy veggies entirely and mass asters with golden creeping Jenny (*Lysimachia nummularia* 'Aurea') to soften the edges of the container.

New Plantings

» **Purple aster**
Aster novi-belgii

WHAT IT IS: perennial
ZONES: 4–8
SWAP OUT: winter

Asters are an outstanding group of fall-blooming perennials. In recent years, they have been bred into something that kind of resembles (and can be sold as a companion or substitute to) the mums found at the fall garden center — big, rounded mounds covered with purple or pink starry blooms. We're not sure how we feel about this, given the natural character of asters, which tends to be lanky, long, and sometimes wandlike. Never mind, the asters we are using here are some derivative of a mass breeding program that decided small is good. In fact, *midget* is good. These colorful little things are just perfect for a blast of color in a container.

INTO THE GARDEN: This is where things can get a little tricky. Many of these asters, like the mums, have been so pampered at the nursery and amped up with so much fertilizer and water that putting them into the garden is a risk. (See Amped-Up Asters, page 106.) Like a junkie without its fix, these plants will often fail in the competitive and less coddled world of the garden. But it's always worth a try. If you find just the right spot — go for more sunshine rather than less — you might end up with a happy aster that grows on to become closer to its true character. You will feel as though you have rescued it from certain death or the compost pile.

ALTERNATIVES: Garden mum (*Chrysanthemum* × *grandiflorum*), Montauk daisy (*Nipponanthemum nipponicum*), Japanese anemone (*Anemone* × *hybrida* 'Little Princess')

Winter

For winter, we adorned the base of the vessel with a garland of boxwood fashioned in a square to complement the shape of the planter. We placed cut redtwig dogwood (*Cornus alba*) sticks in the center of the planting, weaving them in between the azalea's branches. You can stop here if you'd like, or adorn the boxwood base with snippets from the garden. Traditional garden standbys like holly and rose hips work well, or experiment with other textures from your landscape. We used cryptomeria (*Cryptomeria*), pieris (*Pieris*), and skimmia (*Skimmia japonica*).

ADORNMENTS: Fifteen redtwig dogwood branches, 8 sprigs of cryptomeria, 8 sprigs of pieris, 10 sprigs of skimmia with berries, 2 feet of boxwood roping or one 12-inch-square boxwood wreath, 15 sprigs of boxwood

Dressing Up Topiary

SHOULD WE START with our love of topiary or our love of boxwood (*Buxus*)? Let's begin with topiaries, because they led us to boxwood. We fell in love with topiaries soon after we started gardening. Visits to two places got us hooked. The first was Allen Haskell's nursery in New Bedford, Massachusetts, where greenhouse after greenhouse is filled with topiaries, many of them myrtle (*Myrtus*) — our favorite for growing indoors. The second was Tony Elliott's Snug Harbor Farm in Kennebunkport, Maine. To visit Tony and his nursery is to visit a little piece of heaven — chick-ens, black swans, and miniature horses mingle with barns full of handmade terra-cotta. Plants are sold among hornbeam allées and buttresses sculpted from privet, and children are not just welcome but also treated as treasured guests. Best of all are the topiary greenhouses — art-fully filled with topiaries made from ivy, myrtle, mini fuchsias, and pomegranate. Drool. Load on cart. Purchase. Repeat.

Setting aside its formality and association with extrava-gance, topiary in its simplest forms — globes and pyramids — is a lovely addition to any garden, imparting structure and form to a wild perennial border, providing an oasis of green among a bed of riotously colored annuals, or grounding a lofty group of small trees to the earth below them.

And boxwood is the perfect subject. Some boxwood culti-vars tend to grow in a conical, globular, or pyramidal form; nurseries and garden centers take advantage of this trait. Boxwoods that have been care-fully pruned into tidy shapes are expensive because they are slow growers. You can pay someone else to do the prun-ing, or you can buy a young plant and shape it yourself. It just takes time and patience, but the process yields tremendous satisfaction.

DRESSING UP TOPIARY
Spring

The pyramidal boxwood in this planting is the focal point and needs little adornment; to our eyes, it would take away from its beauty and form if there was too much mixed in. So in the spring we decided to stick with greens and golds in similar leaf shapes and sizes. We found lovely pots of mixed sedum with gold, variegated, and green leaves. Their crisp, succulent leaves echo the crispness in shape of the boxwood. The golden creeping Jenny (*Lysimachia nummularia* 'Aurea') helped to soften the planting just a little bit as it draped over the edge of the container.

florist's roses

boxwood

DRESSING UP TOPIARY
Summer

For this season, we wanted to continue in the vein of simple plantings with the boxwood (*Buxus*). We aimed to bring a bit of playfulness to the staid formality of that shrub. We had roses on the brain, pretty pink girly roses, but during a visit to a local (and amazing) rose nursery, we couldn't find any that were small enough to work in the correct scale. Most were grown in a gallon container or bigger, much too big for our needs. Roanne had been at her local grocery store a week before doing the planting and she saw that the store's florist had just brought in a ton of little pink roses in 4-inch containers. They may not be roses we'd choose for our garden, but they were perfect for this container.

DRESSING UP TOPIARY
Fall

As summer turned to autumn, we wanted the accent plants to continue in a soft color palette. We liked the pale, matte cream of the kale, and highlighted it with a garland of shiny violet beautyberries (*Callicarpa*). Draping the beautyberry garland below the edge of the container adds interest and contrast to the crisper, more upright form of the boxwood. The garland also echoes the circular nature of the kale rosettes.

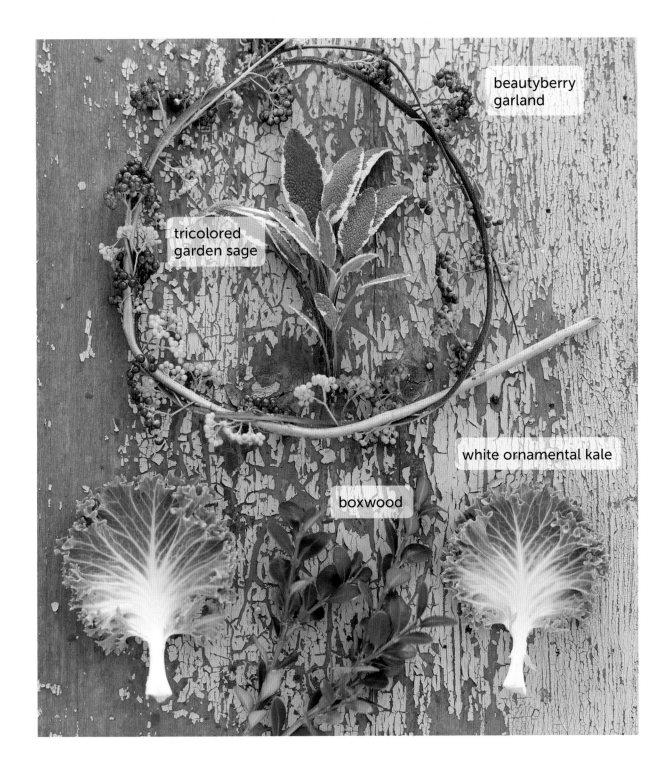

beautyberry garland

tricolored garden sage

white ornamental kale

boxwood

gilded fruits
and vegetables

DRESSING UP TOPIARY
Winter

Boxwood has a regal feel, and its small, glossy leaves are showcased beautifully within the winter landscape. To add an elegant, antique look to the planting, we decided to go for a touch of gold and gild a few fruits and vegetables with gold spray paint.

Metalizing natural elements is a great way to add sparkle to the base of your plantings. Stones, fruit, twigs, veggies, and nuts all can be elevated to golden perfection.

DRESSING UP TOPIARY
PLANT PALETTES

Spring

New Plantings

» **Golden, variegated, and green sedums**
Sedum makinoi
WHAT IT IS: perennial
ZONES: 2–9
SWAP OUT: summer

Sedums are a very useful group of plants, ranging significantly in size, color, and texture. They are tough, cool looking, visually adaptable (meaning they can slide into many planting situations and play different roles), and easy to transplant. They are happiest when planted in full sun in well-drained soil, but they are also content for many years in a container.

INTO THE GARDEN: We took out the sedum for our summer planting but could probably have left it in for one more season. That said, given the formality of the container and its location at the front door, this kind of container is not the one you want to fill with messy, lanky, or wild-looking plants.

When the sedum was taken out, we simply moved it to a sunny, dry bed. It could have also been planted into individual pots and set in a sunny spot. This type of tough sedum thrives in a pot. Sara had one that survived three winters on a Boston roof deck and it came back every spring.

ALTERNATIVES: Euphorbia (*Euphorbia myrsinites*), mini geraniums (*Pelargonium*) with variegated leaves, barrenwort (*Epimedium × youngianum*), thyme (*Thymus vulgaris* 'Aureus' or 'Variegata')

» **Golden creeping Jenny**
Lysimachia nummularia 'Aurea'
WHAT IT IS: perennial
ZONES: 2–9

Despite being a perennial, creeping Jenny has long been used as a container plant, in particular as one that spills and drapes out of a container. The golden color, which is especially strong when it's in full sun — it turns a light chartreuse in part shade and almost pure green in the shade — makes it a great accent plant and provides a bold contrast to many other colors, such as the blues and purples. But be careful; it's long been

known at Sara's house as the golden menace. She planted some in a little foundation bed six or seven years ago, and now it's constantly scheming to take over the lawn.

INTO THE GARDEN: We find this plant to be fairly aggressive. If you like how it looks, keep it as a single specimen in a container. Don't plant it out unless you're prepared to stay constantly on top of its mad march into and around your garden and lawn.

ALTERNATIVES: Chameleon plant (*Houttuynia cordata* 'Chameleon'), periwinkle (*Vinca minor* 'Argentovariegata', *Vinca major* 'Maculata'), box honeysuckle (*Lonicera nitida* 'Baggeson's Gold'), golden oregano (*Origanum vulgare* 'Aureum')

Summer

New Plantings

» **Florist's roses**
Rosa
WHAT IT IS: small shrub, grown as a gift plant
ZONES: unknown
SWAP OUT: fall

These roses sport medium-pink blossoms on very small plants.

Boxwood

FORMED INTO A GLOBE, spiral, or pyramid, boxwood is an excellent container candidate. The container shows off its form, whether run in a group of containers down a walkway, set formally next to a front door, or set in the midst of a cottage garden. And it doesn't take much to keep it happy. Make sure your container has enough drainage holes, water well, feed with diluted organic fertilizer, and prune to keep it shapely. If it's in a small container, you might want to move it inside a cool garage for the winter; but if it's in a larger container like ours, you could wrap it up with burlap if you think wind or snow might be a problem.

The list of cultivars is quite long but filled with treasures, and many are excellent for topiary. For this planting, we used *Buxus sempervirens* 'Suffruticosa'. Among our other favorites are *Buxus sempervirens* 'Green Gem' and *B. s.* 'Green Mountain'.

Zones: 3–8

Site analysis: This large container planting was located at the side of a grand, elegant front door. The garden that surrounds the house is sweeping and manicured in some places but intimate and loose in others. In the garden closest to the front door, there are boxwoods trimmed in tidy shapes and an immaculately groomed privet hedge. The size of the door dictated a large container and a sizable boxwood.

Best containers: Large terra-cotta containers or traditional Williamsburg-style wood boxes with finials

Our container choice: We chose an elegant yet inexpensive white composite container. The size was right for the scale of the door beside which it sits and for the broader landscape. We wanted to see if we could find a container that would *look* expensive even though it wasn't. We planted the boxwood relatively low but with enough room that we could add a textural underplanting each season. We kept the underplantings simple; a few elements were all we needed. Just choosing a few can be tricky, for this style of planting opens itself up to unlimited possibilities.

Alternative plants: Any of a variety of hollies — such as Japanese holly (*Ilex crenata*), American holly (*Ilex opaca*), and English holly (*Ilex aquifolium*) — juniper (*Juniperus*), dwarf Alberta spruce (*Picea glauca* 'Conica'), yew (*Taxus*)

DRESSING UP TOPIARY
PLANT PALETTES

These are intended as one-season wonders; best to treat them as annuals.

INTO THE GARDEN: These grocers' roses (as we're calling them — not sure of their species) are very needy. They've likely been brought to the point of perfect beauty with lots of water, lots of fertilizer, and lots of pesticides. With a cool greenhouse, maybe they could be brought in during the cold weather and carried through the winter in individual pots with a good deal of care and attention. We think the best thing to do is to take them out of the container after the summer season, pot them up into little terra-cotta pots, and use them as a centerpiece for a party or on an outdoor picnic table and bench.

ALTERNATIVES: Garden pinks (*Dianthus*, for example, *Dianthus* 'Tiny Rubies'), ornamental strawberry (*Fragaria* 'Pink Panda'), impatiens (*Impatiens*), oenothera (*Oenothera speciosa* 'Rosea'), verbena (*Verbena* × *hybrida* 'Sissinghurst')

Fall

New Plantings

» White ornamental kale
Brassica oleracea
WHAT IT IS: ornamental annual vegetable
ZONES: n/a
SWAP OUT: winter

Ornamental kales and cabbages have become a welcome staple in autumn nurseries and garden centers. The range of offerings is growing, too; there are large ones that are more than 2 feet in diameter, tiny ones that are less than 6 inches in diameter, smooth-leaved ones, and frilly leaved ones. They come mostly in shades of purple and white with green on the edges. They are annual vegetables, so they do not continue on after this season. They do well in sun or part shade and in evenly moist soil.

INTO THE GARDEN: Because we wanted to completely change the look of this container for winter, we took out these kales at the end of autumn. You could leave them in, maybe with a false wreath around the base with a purple ribbon or other magenta- and mauve-toned decoration. This is assuming

the kale has stayed in good shape; if it hasn't, yank it and throw it on the compost pile or feed it to your chickens.

ALTERNATIVES: Aster (*Aster novi-belgii*), bergenia (*Bergenia cordifolia*), bugleweed (*Ajuga* 'Silver Queen'), 'Bright Lights' Swiss chard (*Beta vulgaris* 'Bright Lights')

» Tricolored garden sage
Salvia officinalis 'Tricolor'
WHAT IT IS: perennial
ZONES: 4–8
SWAP OUT: winter

This herb-garden regular is as adaptable and beautiful in the ornamental garden as it is delicious when fried up and served with ravioli. This particular cultivar, with its white and green, bumpy, 3- to 4-inch-long leaves held up by soft-lilac stems, is a perfect mixer in many a container but looks especially good with this scrumptious purple palette. Sages like it on the dry, sunny, and hot side of things, so be sure to use a light potting mix when filling in the spaces around this planting. This will enable you to water enough to keep the boxwood happy but still have the upper layer of soil well drained.

INTO THE GARDEN: Rather than plant it out, we used the sage for Thanksgiving turkey stuffing. Yum!

ALTERNATIVES: Heuchera (*Heuchera* 'Quicksilver'), hellebore (*Helleborus* 'Sunshine Selections'), lamb's ear (*Stachys byzantina*), foamflower (*Tiarella* 'Mint Chocolate')

ADORNMENTS: Garland with purple beautyberries (*Callicarpa dichotoma* or *C. japonica*). Beautyberry is a charming smallish shrub that spends most of the year quietly supporting the other stars of the garden with its simple structure of green foliage and tiny, insignificant flowers. Come fall, however, the small clusters of purple berries begin to ripen as the turning foliage falls away. The berries become one of the stars of the fall garden. Such a fabulous color is hard to find in the garden at this time of year.

The cut branches of berries don't last a terribly long time in this composition (two weeks). As soon as they begin to look tired and the berries start to wrinkle and fall off, take them out and replace them with freshly cut stems or simply leave the container with just the kale and sage.

Winter

In the winter landscape, we thought our topiary would look great rimmed with a Williamsburg-style treatment of gilded pears, artichokes, and bay leaves that we constructed in a sturdy foam wreath form placed around the base of the planting. Gilding is an easy and festive way to create seasonal adornments; for more information, read How to Gild, below.

How to Gild

FROM A DISTANCE, spray paint looks just as nice as traditional gilding (which is usually accomplished with sheets of gold leaf that are adhered to objects with a coating of gelatin). Spray painting is quick and requires less of an investment in materials. There are all sorts of tones of golds and silvers to experiment with, from milky platinum, to antiqued gold to pearlized blue. Try spraying on multiple layers for a glossy, glasslike presentation, or try a quick coat for a look that's more like a patina or glaze.

When working with fruit or nuts, first stake the materials by either piercing or drilling a hole and inserting a small stake or skewer. Place staked objects in a foam board and spray them according to the directions on the can of paint, as well as your own aesthetic sense. Let the objects dry completely before adding them to your design.

To create the base for your gilded adornments, use a sturdy foam wreath form. For our topiary planting, we left the fruit and vegetables on their stakes after painting and simply inserted them into the form, using bay leaves to fill any gaps we found.

A Shrub for All Seasons

THERE ARE A tremendous number of lovely spring-blooming woody plants that are excellent candidates for a container specimen. We like to use plants that will be interesting to look at from season to season and not just be one-hit wonders, so we always try to find plants with great summer foliage, colorful berries, interesting seedheads, or even unusual bark. Many spring-blooming shrubs also have a sweet fragrance that entices the pollinators. We like having these fragrant plants growing on well-worn paths so that we can appreciate them daily.

One of our favorite places to visit in springtime is Harvard University's Arnold Arboretum, in Jamaica Plain, Massachusetts. Every week, one can find dozens of interesting new trees and shrubs bursting into bloom. Outside the Hunnewell building is a mass of pale, gray-stemmed shrubs whose frothy, greenish white blossoms are abuzz with apian activity. On a warm day, the air is adrift with a sweet, light honey fragrance. Since we first had this delightful springtime experience, we've seen fothergilla in many more places in and around New England; thank goodness, because what a glut of great characteristics are packed into this one little shrub. You can't help but be almost dorkily cheery when you see one.

Even before the warm sun brings out the honey-scented blossoms, the tight buds are simply delightful to look at, especially up close. They look like tiny pale green pinecones. They seem to last for at least a month before they open into sweet bottlebrush flowers. The creamy flowers, their fragrance, and the happy bees linger for about two weeks before the leaves begin to arrive on the shrub, unfurling just in time to hide the declining flowers. The leaves are a pleasant green, or, if you find the cultivar 'Blue Mist', a glaucous blue-green shade. But summer is the shrub's quiet season, for with autumn arrives a riot of orange, red, and yellow foliage that hangs on for ages. Don't expect this amazing mix of colors every year, though; sometimes they're all bright yellow, sometimes yellow with an edge of red, and sometimes a deeper burgundy red. All are beautiful and long lasting. These amazing seasonal contributions are the reason we chose the fothergilla as our spring-blooming-shrub backbone.

A SHRUB FOR ALL SEASONS
Spring

The underplanting in this container was designed to highlight and play off the sweet greeny yellow-white bottlebrush flowers of the fothergilla. The blossoms give the plant a delicate air, which is a contrast to the leaves that come later. The flowers of the daffodil mingle in the branches of the fothergilla, bridging the gap between the underplant and the upper reaches of the shrub, where many of its flowers form. The leaves of both the lungwort and the sweet woodruff give a crisp texture to the under-planting through much of the spring and into the early summer. The lungwort's blue flowers are a stunning contrast with both the daffodils and the fothergilla when they overlap bloom time. We added Irish moss to provide quiet places for the eye to rest and admire the subtle beauty of the container itself.

'E.B. Anderson'
lungwort

'Minnow'
daffodil

sweet woodruff

Irish moss

fothergilla
buds

sweet
woodruff

'Cat's Eye' hosta

'Limey Lisa'
hosta

lilyturf

self-heal

Japanese
false nettle

fothergilla

A SHRUB FOR ALL SEASONS
Summer

Because summer is a quieter time for fothergilla, we thought it would be fun to amp up the wattage with the underplanting. The excitement in this planting comes almost entirely from a cool world of greens and, of course, from texture. The two hostas — one miniature and pure gold, the other a medium-size one with strong golden variegation — provide bold blocks of color and texture with their corrugated leaves. Self-heal (*Prunella*) with its small but plentiful scalloped leaves, was added as a textural contrast. False nettle, with its leaves that range in color from bright chartreuse to deep green speckled with lime, was used to bridge the color gaps among the bold and gold of the hostas, the pure green of the self-heal, and the backbone plant itself. Finally, the lovely, stripey, gold-and-green lilyturf (*Liriope*) provides fireworks, both in shape and color. From a distance, it reads as almost white, though on closer inspection it is in fact golden as well.

Twelve Containers through the Year

A SHRUB FOR ALL SEASONS
Fall

Autumn is a magical time of year in the garden, especially if you've added some smart shrubs to your plantings. Fothergilla is one of the most beautiful fall players, adding orange, red, yellow, and even burgundy foliage to the bigger picture. Our fothergilla decided to color up late and stayed on the burgundy and yellow side of things. We added only one new member to the summer troop — bunchberry (*Cornus canadensis*). We liked the way it echoed the ruby tones of the fothergilla. All the other plants, with the exception of the sweet woodruff (*Galium odoratum*), added gold and yellow in varying shades, lighting up the fothergilla's feet. Sweet woodruff did her sweet little thing and gave us a quiet green place to rest our eyes.

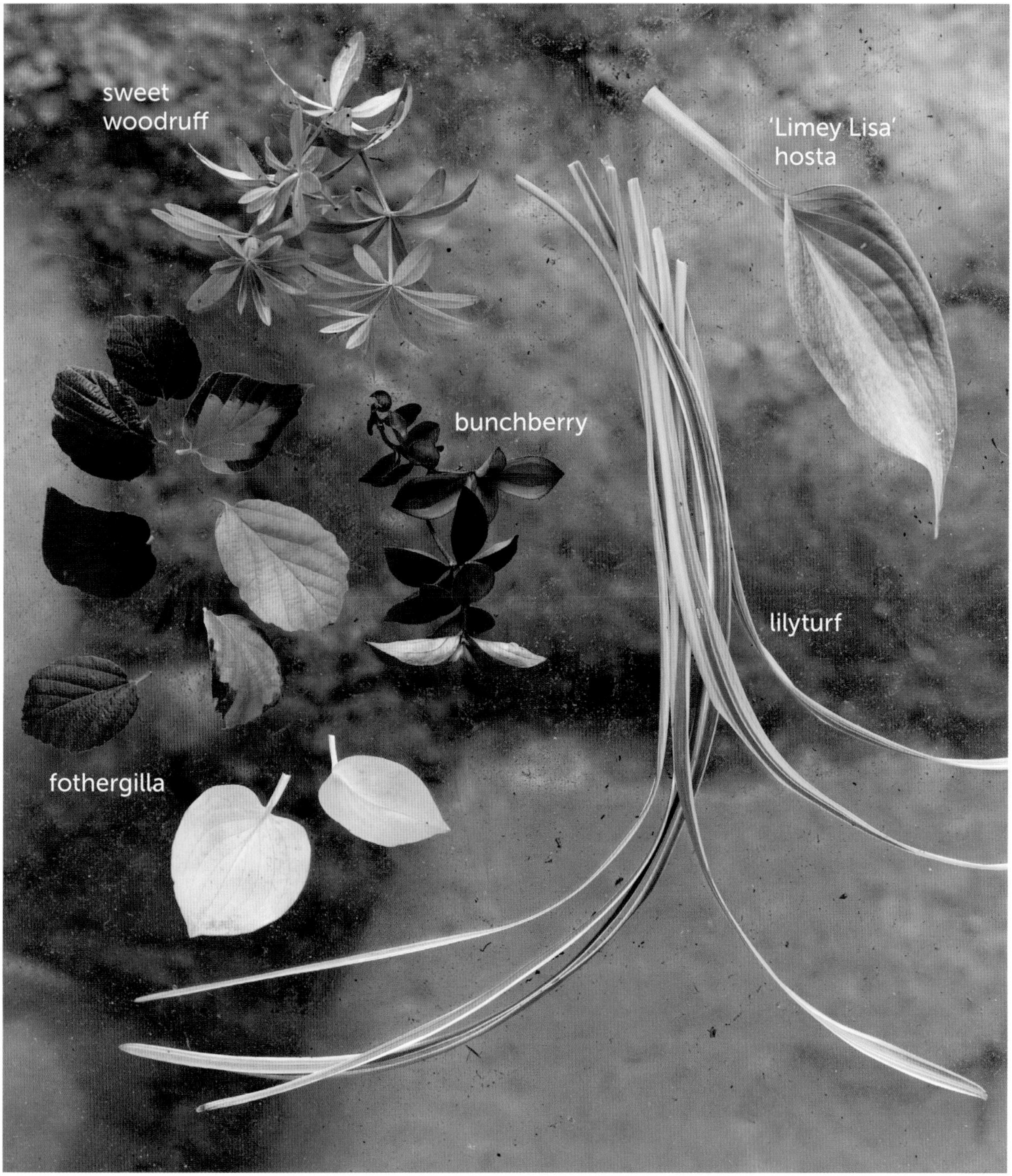

sweet
woodruff

'Limey Lisa'
hosta

bunchberry

lilyturf

fothergilla

ornaments for the birds

A SHRUB FOR ALL SEASONS
Winter

In thinking about how to decorate this planting for the winter, we decided it would be fun to create something that would be as appealing for the birds as it was for ourselves — a birdseed-encrusted wreath! Its lovely, subtle colors and interesting texture look great under fothergilla's intricate web of branches and plays nicely with the aged cast-stone vessel. To top it off, we decorated the branches with the birdseed-and-bean ornaments that our kids, Alex, Jack, and Nora, helped make one snowy morning in December. Happy holidays to our fine feathered friends — they keep life going in our gardens year after year!

Purple Deluxe

WHO DOESN'T COVET a little bit of purple? We all do — it is dark and mysterious, rich and regal. Purple leaves are a delight to use in garden design because they are a foil for brighter colors, like gold and red (think of *Dahlia* 'Bishop of Llandaff' — bright red flowers and deep purple leaves), which really make them pop. You can also use it as a complement to subtler colors like the silvers, maroons, burgundies, browns, and greens we featured in our container. Setting a whole container full of purple-leaved plants against a gray backdrop like this old barn also makes a big impact.

Our backbone plant here, the very classic and easy-to-find 'Bloodgood' Japanese maple (*Acer palmatum* 'Bloodgood'), has leaves that are closer to the burgundy red spectrum of purple. Certainly don't limit yourself to this cultivar unless you adore it, since saying there's an abundance of gorgeous Japanese maple cultivars available is a huge understatement. Plant what you love, paying close attention not only to tree shape, leaf color and form but also to bark — many of them have elegant and colorful branches, while the mature trunks are a soft gray. Be sure to explore the vast range of new plants with purple foliage in the market today. Whereas it used to be difficult to find a purple-leaved tree or shrub (other than purple sand cherry

or copper beech), now the options are much greater. We particularly love the purple smokebush (*Cotinus coggygria* 'Royal Velvet' or 'Velvet Cloak'). Purple redbud (*Cercis canadensis* 'Forest Pansy') is a gorgeous cultivar; it grows a bit more slowly and with slightly fewer blossoms, but is entirely worth it for the foliage. Look for purple-leaved crab apples, too, for a bit of a twist on a classic.

Among the shrubs, we especially love purple ninebark (*Physocarpus* 'Summer Wine'), the cutleaf elderberries (like *Sambucus* 'Eva'), and *Weigela* 'Midnight Wine' and 'Wine and Roses'. All make lovely container specimens and will thrive in the garden when planted out.

PURPLE DELUXE
Spring

We know that purple and green look good together in the garden, but we wanted to try a more unusual palette for this container. The brown pot dictated many of our decisions, leading us in the direction of darker silver, eggplant-purple, and brown. If we'd chosen a silver or gray vessel, we might have selected a more shimmery, silvery palette. Since our backbone plant is bare during spring, we wanted to bring the suggestion of its future leaves down into the underplanting using the dark heuchera, deep purple pansy, and the black mondo grass (*Ophiopogon*). At the same time, we wanted it to have a cheery spring feel, so we used the pale, pretty tricolored sage and white-and-violet pansy to evoke that.

black mondo
grass

tricolored
garden sage

pansies

'Palace Purple'
heuchera

Japanese maple

'Bloodgood'
Japanese maple

microbiota

'Palace Purple'
heuchera

weeping brown
sedge

PURPLE DELUXE
Summer

By summer, the elegant, fan-like leaves of the Japanese maple (*Acer palmatum* 'Bloodgood') have filled in. This season and the next are when this backbone plant shines, so we wanted to keep underplantings fairly simple and straightforward. Working in broad brushstrokes, we used three plants, each one a different color. We could have just as easily planted a large mound of moss and left it at that, which would have been fitting and respectful of the quiet beauty of a Japanese maple.

PURPLE DELUXE
Fall

Here we've kept the composition simple, shifting the elements around and adding one shiny, happy berried plant for a bit of early-fall sparkle. Despite our lack of new plants, there is a lot of motion and texture in the composition, which is delightfully evocative of Japanese calligraphy. This maple colors up well in late autumn, giving a blast of reddish purple just before the snow arrives.

in containers. Their range of colors is staggering and on almost all accounts delicious. It seems like more cool ones are released every year. Their general size and leaf shape are perfect for popping in here and there, adding texture and color where we need it. They seem to thrive in a mixed container setting, which is funny because we can't seem to keep them happy in a pot on their own. We used 'Palace Purple' because it is a classic and particularly easy to find at most nurseries, but try any of them wherever you can fit them in. Most plantings are better for the addition of a heuchera or two or five. Among our favorites are the silver and burgundy ones — 'Quilter's Joy', 'Pewter Moon', 'Silver Scrolls', and 'Amethyst Myst'. Ro loves some of the more caramelly ones, like 'Crème Brûlée' and 'Amber Waves'. Their only downside is that some of them seem to melt away in the garden; we just experiment and see what works.

INTO THE GARDEN: These plants don't mind staying in a container, provided they receive a happy mix of part

'Bloodgood' Japanese maple

JAPANESE MAPLES ARE particularly well suited to container life, evoking as they do the elegant and quietly beautiful art of bonsai. Although not quite as small as bonsai, many young Japanese maples (which are best for containers) are still almost perfectly proportioned miniature trees, and it's fun to create a little woodland world around one. This is great for families with young children.

Japanese maples require rich, moist but well-drained soil, and sun to part shade. If you want to keep your tree in a container for a couple of years, you will need to prune it to keep it at a reasonable size. There are a number of excellent cultivars to choose from; we've selected *Acer palmatum* 'Bloodgood'.

Zones: 3–8

Site analysis: This container was placed at the side door of a gray antique barn. We loved the browns, purples, silvers, and grays against the austere, vertical barn boards.

Best containers: Terra-cotta rolled-rim pot; simple wooded box with planks running vertically; tall, slender, aged metal or zinc cylindrical vessel

Our container choice: We chose a large brown, molded plastic container because we really liked the color. It was big but lightweight and durable.

Alternative plants: Elderberry (*Sambucus* 'Black Lace'), smokebush (*Cotinus* 'Royal Purple'), redbud (*Cercis* 'Forest Pansy'), weeping copper beech (*Fagus* 'Purpurea Pendula')

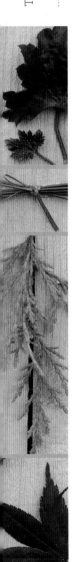

PURPLE DELUXE
PLANT PALETTES

shade, average moisture, and fertile soil. We left 'Palace Purple' in the container from spring right through until fall and then simply planted it out into the garden. Make sure you really firm the soil around them when planting, especially if you're planting them in the fall, and finish up with a mulch — otherwise, they tend to heave themselves out of the ground during the winter.

ALTERNATIVES: Heuchera (*Heuchera* 'Quilter's Joy', 'Frosted Violet', or 'Midnight Burgundy'), Labrador violet (*Viola labradorica*)

» ## Black mondo grass
Ophiopogon planiscapus 'Nigrescens'
WHAT IT IS: perennial
ZONES: 6–11
SWAP OUT: summer

This dark, slender, grasslike plant is fabulously mysterious. Why? Well, for starters, botanists only recently realized that it wasn't a lilyturf at all and gave it its own delicious name, which sounds like a wizard from *Harry*

Potter. And its color is so very, very close to black that it seems plantalogically wrong yet so right. It has little purple flowers that dangle prettily from the flower stalk and then agreeably turn into violet-black berries. Mostly it wants to be grown in average soil and part shade; add some moisture when the high and dry summertime rolls around. And for lawd's sake, plant some snowdrops (*Galanthus*) in among the dark clumps! Deluxe.

INTO THE GARDEN: We moved it into the garden: It's most lovely at the edge of a bed, where it can be noticed. If set too far back, it will get lost, be sad, and probably die, just to spite you. As with anything being moved in the summer, be generous with lots of moisture for the first month or so in its new home. Moisture is important to these plants, so if you can't find a spot in the garden immediately, be sure to keep it moist until you're able to plant it into the garden.

ALTERNATIVES: There are really none; but for a grassy feel, try lilyturf (*Liriope muscari*).

Summer

Holdovers from Spring

» ### 'Palace Purple' heuchera
Heuchera 'Palace Purple'

Stays that yummy deep rich purple, echoing the maple's leaves.

New Plantings

» ## Weeping brown sedge
Carex flagellifera
WHAT IT IS: perennial
ZONES: (5) 6–9
SWAP OUT: fall or winter

These brown New Zealand sedges are some of the loveliest, if difficult to get used to, additions to the plant market in the past few years. Only on the border of hardiness for many of us, they're still pretty irresistible, and they make excellent container plants. Once you start using these bronze, grasslike plants, you will want to use them all over the place. Weeping brown sedge (*Carex flagellifera*) is one of the hardier bronze sedges, but if you'd like to try others (which you should), try hair sedge (*C. comans* cultivars) and leatherleaf sedge (*C. buchananii*). Keep in mind that these two, particularly *C. comans,* are not fond of winter snow and ice. All of them prefer moist but well-drained soil and full sun.

INTO THE GARDEN: These look splendid in the garden and in a container on their own. You can move them into either place and they'll be quite happy, as long as you give them sufficient moisture — but then again, if they die, who will know? We kept ours as part of the underplanting right through until the winter change-out and it was as happy as a clam.

ALTERNATIVES: Hair sedge (*Carex comans* 'Dancing Flame' or *C. comans* 'Frosted Curls'), leatherleaf sedge (*C. buchananii*)

» Microbiota
Microbiota decussata
WHAT IT IS: shrub
ZONES: 2–7
SWAP OUT: spring

This bright green, low-growing (12–18 inches) shrub is the refined cousin of the juniper; the growth habit is slightly more delicate and lacy, and it turns a muted but pretty purple-bronze in the winter. Also, this plant doesn't seem to irritate your skin in the way junipers can. Microbiota is native to Siberia, which makes it hardy to Zone 2. It's pretty easygoing, requiring full sun to part shade and well-drained but otherwise average soil. The only thing that seems to upset it is too much heat and humidity.

INTO THE GARDEN: Because it's so hardy, we could have kept it happily contained right through until spring. If you plant it out into the garden, provide good moisture and part shade if you live on the warmer end of the hardiness zones. Otherwise, let him rip.

ALTERNATIVES: 'Bar Harbor' juniper (*Juniperus* 'Bar Harbor'), Japanese painted fern (*Athyrium niponicum* 'Pictum'), sensitive fern (*Onoclea sensibilis*)

Fall

Holdovers from Summer

» Microbiota
Microbiota descussata
This hardy, frothy shrub stays crisply bright green right through until the onset of consistent frosts.

» Weeping brown sedge
Carex flagellifera

This is where tough choices come in. This carex looks pretty, fluid, and beige all the way through the fall. The problem is that we've had trouble over-wintering it, even in the garden, if we plant it late in the fall. So your choices are as follows: Plant out after the fall change-out, keep it well watered, and have a good chance of it settling in and surviving the winter. Or leave it in to be beautiful through the autumn, plant it out in late fall, mulch it well (3–4 inches), and hope for the best.

» 'Palace Purple' heuchera
Heuchera 'Palace Purple'

Old steady Eddie, he just keeps providing that deep, rich purple.

New Plants for Fall

» Cranberry cotoneaster
Cotoneaster apiculatus
WHAT IT IS: shrub
ZONES: 4–7
SWAP OUT: spring

This stiffly branched, low-growing shrub is a terrific addition to garden and container because of its coarse

PURPLE DELUXE
PLANT PALETTES

Winter

growth habit and its berries. The berries are bright red and last until at least mid-November. The foliage is also attractive, with its small, glossy, wavy leaves lining branches that seem to have a mind of their own. Best grown in full sun or partial shade and in well-drained soil, cotoneasters as a rule are always happy to drape themselves in a stylish fashion down the sides of retaining walls and terraces and containers.

INTO THE GARDEN: We kept cotoneaster in the container with the maple and the micro-biota until spring, pulling it out once the container was thawed out. If you want to take it out and plant it in the garden sooner, be sure to keep it well watered until winter comes and give it a 3- to 4-inch layer of mulch to prevent heaving during the freezing and thawing cycle.

ALTERNATIVES: Rockspray cotoneaster (*Cotoneaster horizontalis*), firethorn (*Pyracantha coccinea* 'Orange'), bearberry (*Arctostaphylos uva-ursi*)

» 'Jervis' Canadian hemlock
Tsuga canadensis 'Jervis'
WHAT IT IS: conifer
ZONES: 4–8
SWAP OUT: spring

'Jervis' is a slow-growing, densely branched, dwarf hemlock. His irregular but elegant growth habit, evergreen foliage, and purple-tinted bark makes him a great addition to any landscape, and a fantastic conifer for containers. He grows 3 to 6 inches per year and responds well to a good clipping. He would also be an interesting character in a mini conifer landscape or planted among other mini conifers in a natural stone trough.

INTO THE GARDEN: In spring or fall, plant 'Jervis' in full sun to shade. He prefers a cool, moist climate and well-drained soils that are rich in organic matter.

ALTERNATIVES: Other conifers with unique forms, like *Chamaecyparis obtusa* 'Contorta' or 'Little Ann', gold-kissed *C. o.* 'Meroke', or deep

green *Ilex crenata* 'Dwarf Pagoda'

» 'Golden Sprite' dwarf Hinoki cypress
Chamaecyparis obtusa 'Golden Sprite'
WHAT IT IS: conifer
ZONES: 5–8
SWAP OUT: fall or spring

One of the smallest golden Hinoki cypresses, this dwarf conifer grows very slowly into a sweet little golden bun. Its little fans of foliage develop sunny yellow tips that vary in intensity. We chose this colorful sprite to drive the color story of our container. She can take partial shade, but without full sun her coloration will be more subtle. Avoid planting her in full sun in hot climates, for her leaves will scorch.

INTO THE GARDEN: Like most mini conifers, 'Golden Sprite' prefers moist, well-drained soil. You can keep this plant in the container for an indefinite period of time or you can plant her out to the garden in spring or fall, among other conifer beauties, heath and heathers, and sweet little thymes.

ALTERNATIVES: Other golden conifer selections like *Chamaecyparis pisifera* 'Mops' or other tiny conifer buns like *Chamaecyparis obtusa* 'Nana', *Chamaecyparis obtusa* 'Gnome' or *Picea abies* 'Fat Cat'

» 'Dainty Doll' dwarf Hinoki cypress
Chamaecyparis obtusa 'Dainty Doll'

WHAT IT IS: conifer
ZONES: 5–8
SWAP OUT: fall or spring

'Dainty Doll' is one of the more charming dwarf Hinoki cypresses. Her lacy, deep green foliage and low, rounded habit bring some bulk to the base of the underplanting. As 'Dainty Doll' matures she loses her plump baby figure and shifts to a more irregular form that becomes wider than tall. Her true green foliage pairs nicely with both deep burgundy tones (like those in leucothoe) or with golden tones like the ones we used in this underplanting.

INTO THE GARDEN: This is an excellent candidate for long-term container growing, but could also be planted out to the garden in fall or spring. Plant it in moist, well-drained soil, in sun to partial shade. 'Dainty Doll' will grow about 3 to 6 inches per year and in the ground can mature to about 4 feet tall.

ALTERNATIVES: Mix up this combination by trying new textures like *Pinus densifolia* 'Low Glow' or *Cryptomeria japonica* 'Elegans Nana'. A broadleaf evergreen like a dwarf pieris could be fun too; we especially like *Pieris japonica* 'Cavatine'.

» Blue nest spruce
Picea mariana 'Ericoides'

WHAT IS IT: conifer
ZONES: 3–8
SWAP OUT: fall or spring

The silvery blue tones of 'Ericoides' bring a welcome contrast to this combination, lending an icy feel to the base of the planting and playing off the yellow highlights of 'Golden Sprite'. 'Ericoides' is a low-maintenance, slow-growing conifer,

reaching 3 feet tall and 4 to 5 feet wide. Plant him anywhere you need a nice dense globe of texture.

INTO THE GARDEN: Plant 'Ericoides' in well-drained acid soils in partial to full sun. In the garden or in the container, 'Ericoides' is a great companion plant; his silver-toned texture looks great planted among purple-toned foliage.

ALTERNATIVES: *Picea omorika* 'Kamenz', *Picea pungens* 'Waldbrunn', *Juniperus squamata* 'Blue Star', or *Calluna vulgaris* 'Silver Queen'

ADORNMENTS: Branches of Atlantic white cedar, leucothoe, pinecones, and tree lichens

Woodland Shrubbery

THE AREAS OF the garden that dwell between shade and sun can be some of the most difficult spots to find plants for. In the spring, the garden can be bright and sunny, whereas in high summer, the canopy of mature trees may have closed in, so plants formerly growing in full sun are now cast into the shade. There are many permutations of "partial shade," so defining it can't be difficult. A partial-shade garden might be bathed in the hot summer sun for one hour and spend the rest of the day in full shade. Or it might be pleasantly dappled all day long (which is often the best scenario to have).

Once you embrace the partial-shade areas of your garden and begin to hunt for appropriate plants, you'll find that your choice is much broader and richer than you anticipated. The areas of partial shade have the potential to become the lushest, most verdant parts of your garden, and the ones where the seasons are most apparent.

We like to grow shrubs that walk that fine line between sun and shade, and we've found that the plants that prefer woodland edge–type habitat — where one foot is in the field and one in the forest — do best. These shrubs do well in a range of light levels, perhaps growing bigger and more lustily in full sun but attaining a more delicate and simple beauty on the shady end of the spectrum. And we find that because they're so culturally adaptable, they're also visually adaptable to a range of underplantings. We selected the oakleaf hydrangea (*Hydrangea quercifolia*) because of its irresistible foliage as well as its lovely blooms and snappy bark, which curls and softly peels off mature stems.

WOODLAND SHRUBBERY
Spring

For this planting, we wanted to set a dramatic stage for the year to come. With this planting placed in a spot with dappled shade, spring was the only time of year when we felt that we could go a bit more toward the dark side of the palette — the spring sun was so bright and abundant. At this point in the year, the new leaves of the oakleaf hydrangea are so delicate looking: light green with white fuzzy undersides. We contrasted this lightness with the deep, dark purple-black violets (*Viola*) — lots of them. The visual relief comes from the barrenwort (*Epimedium*), whose pale violet-and-white blooms stand out against the dark violas. The crisply shaped leaves of the globe flower and the lacy foliage of the stinking hellebore add texture to the composition.

'Rose Queen'
barrenwort

oakleaf hydrangea

'Lemon Queen'
globe flower

stinking
hellebore

'Bowles Black'
violet

Japanese fountain grass

'Quicksilver' foamflower

crested lady fern

oakleaf hydrangea

'Hadspen Cream' bugloss

WOODLAND SHRUBBERY
Summer

With the arrival of summer, the sun becomes shaded out as the vines climbing the deck grow lusher. We wanted the container to become more of a bright spot in this grottolike nook. The brightest "lights" come from the oakleaf's big, creamy white blossoms up high, which are grounded to the container with the crisp white edging of the variegated bugloss foliage. The tiny white starlike flowers of the foam-flower are a pretty accent, and we love this plant's subtle variegation, which becomes more important later in the summer. The lovely Japanese fountain grass is like the sun's rays pouring out over the side of the container. It adds golden warmth and movement with its grassy blades.

WOODLAND SHRUBBERY
Fall

You almost don't need to talk about design thoughts for this season; you could simply leave the oakleaf hydrangea to stand alone without anything planted beneath it other than moss — it is that handsome! But we love plants and we couldn't resist the call of the bright red Bowman's root (*Gillenia trifoliata*) as a companion. We also tucked in a few golden yellow sedges (*Carex pensylvanica*), which helped pick up the occasional yellow tones in the Bowman's root and added a textural quality to the planting. The sedge gave the whole composition a bit of movement and light. It also helped the container connect to the marshy grass and brackish inlet/river that this property looks out to.

'Rose Queen'
barrenwort

oakleaf hydrangea

Pennsylvania sedge

Bowman's root

oakleaf
hydrangea

sumac

leucothoe

dwarf Siberian
spruce

boxwood

Winter

Oakleaf hydrangea's great bark is showcased again; in winter months, the branches seem to have a mahogany shine to them. To complement this, we decided on a tonal arrangement of red-hued conifers and woodland shrubs. For a festive twist, we nestled in some sumac stems; their burgundy seed heads were just the ticket.

WOODLAND SHRUBBERY PLANT PALETTES

Spring

New Plantings

» 'Lemon Queen' globe flower
Trollius × *cultorum* 'Lemon Queen'
WHAT IT IS: perennial
ZONES: 3–7
SWAP OUT: summer

This moisture-loving perennial has dissected leaves that are a strong, textural backdrop for the charming, buttercup-like flowers. Its leaves are the main draw because although lovely, the flowers last a very short time.

INTO THE GARDEN: Happy as long as you keep up with their moisture needs, the globe flowers can be a nice addition to the full-sun to part-shade border where you need a bit of long-lasting green texture. They're a great addition to a bog garden (yup, they like that much water), and they won't spread the way some of the other members of the ranunculus family do. Many globe flowers are too boldly colored to combine with a subtle planting like this one, but the lemon yellow of this cultivar's flowers is an easy mixer. Globe flowers would be content staying in a container all year — again, given sufficient moisture.

ALTERNATIVES: Hardy geraniums (*Geranium sanguineum* 'Album', *Geranium phaeum* 'Album'), geum (*Geum*), masterwort (*Astrantia* subsp. *involucrata* 'Shaggy'), wood anemone (*Anemone nemorosa* 'Vestal')

» 'Bowles Black' violet
Viola 'Bowles Black'
WHAT IT IS: perennial
ZONES: 5–8
SWAP OUT: summer

Sweet, small-flowered violets in a dark, mysterious color are a treasure in the garden and in containers, especially when planted en masse. Their little yellow eye is like a warm glowing light in the dark forest. They bloom for a long period, provided the temperatures don't get too warm too quickly and they're kept deadheaded.

INTO THE GARDEN: We took it out of the container and simply composted it because, despite being listed as a perennial, both of us have had a hard time getting it and other "perennial" violas to come back a second year. That said, it may be worth leaving it in and seeing what happens for you. Also, it often self-sows, so keep your eyes peeled for baby Bowles. Don't forget to pick little bouquets of this lovely flower during the peak blooming season; it will keep him blooming heavily. If you keep him in the container for the following season, just be sure to keep deadheading.

ALTERNATIVES: Nemesia (*Nemesia fruticans*), violet (*Viola*, in one color), bugleweed (*Ajuga* 'Caitlin's Giant'), dwarf crested iris (*Iris cristata*)

» 'Rose Queen' barrenwort
Epimedium grandiflorum 'Rose Queen'
WHAT IT IS: perennial
ZONES: 4–8
SWAP OUT: winter

This diminutive but stately ground cover is a must-have for containers and gardens alike. The foliage is the main draw, with shieldlike leaves emerging with flushes of bronzy red that eventually end up green as the gardening season marches on. A pleasing bonus is the sweet pinky rose blossoms that dangle from slender stems in the spring, like fantastical little lanterns.

INTO THE GARDEN: We left our barrenwort in place until late November and then we planted it into the garden. Late fall is a good time to plant them out because the soil is moist and their roots get a good start before the heat returns. If you move them to the garden during the summer, be sure to keep them well watered through the fall. Barrenworts prefer a shady spot in humus-rich, moist, well-drained soil. They will tolerate drought if they are well established.

ALTERNATIVES: Barrenworts (*Epimedium* 'Cherry Tart', *Epimedium × youngianum* 'Roseum'), fernleaf bleeding heart (*Dicentra* 'King of Hearts'), rue anemone (*Anemonella thalictroides* 'Schoaff's Double'), pink lily of the valley (*Convallaria majalis* 'Rosea')

Oakleaf hydrangea

AYE . . . THE HYDRANGEA CLAN, such an impressive one. Many of us know this genus from the billowing, flouncy blue mophead hydrangea (*Hydrangea macrophylla*) that everyone covets but few of us grow well. Elegant, colorful flowers to be sure. One member of the clan not to miss is the oakleaf hydrangea (*Hydrangea quercifolia*). To meet him is to fall in love with him. We chose this plant because it, like many of our other backbone plants, has magnetic qualities that unfold season to season, each greater than the last.

Oakleaf hydrangeas are best grown in full sun to part shade with substantial moisture and rich, well-drained soil. You can prune if you feel that it's growing out of bounds, but this is a plant that seems to know itself well, and its strong character is best shown when left to its own devices.

When you buy an oakleaf hydrangea at the nursery, take your time and be sure to get one with a well-balanced framework of branches. One of its best traits, the wiry, almost bendy-looking branches, can also be its downfall. Many nurseries sell plants that have awkward shapes; keep looking until you find the perfect plant. There are several excellent cultivars on the market worth searching out; two favorites are 'Snowflake', whose flowers look doubled, and 'Snow Queen', whose fall color is a bright red.

Zones: 5–9

Site analysis: This container was placed below a deck, near the ocean, providing a bright spot for house guests on their way to the outdoor shower.

Best containers: Simple aged terra-cotta, zinc or stick/wood rustic container

Our container choice: We chose a very simple but visually strong container in a classic shape. The vessel is a very neutral concrete gray to complement the stone in the nearby areas. It was slightly wider than it was high, which helped it to support the shallow roots of the hydrangea as well as to provide enough space to accommodate the root balls of large-sized perennials.

Alternative plants: Grape holly (*Mahonia bealii* or *M. aquifolium*); summersweet (*Clethra alnifolia* 'Ruby Spice'), red buckeye (*Aesculus pavia*)

WOODLAND SHRUBBERY
PLANT PALETTES

» **Stinking hellebore**
Helleborus foetidus
WHAT IT IS: perennial
ZONES: 6–9
SWAP OUT: summer

An excellent addition to the helleborophile's garden, the stinking hellebore has tall stalks that hold up to 40 green flowers per stem in mid-spring, but it is the slightly toothed palm-shaped leaves that make it a plant worth keeping through the year. It prefers part shade with a nice, rich soil; it grows well in dry shade if given sufficient water as it establishes itself. *H. foetidus* 'Red Silver' is a striking version of this plant, with silver-gray leaf markings and red stems.

INTO THE GARDEN: What you do with your contained hellebore afterward depends on how big a plant you used and whether it came from a nursery or your garden. They can grow quite big in the garden and seed around, which makes them perfect for digging up and tucking into a container. A season in a container, however, can be tough on a dug-up plant, so water it well after replanting and check on it regularly. If you bought it from a nursery, it will be happy to be replanted once the spring season is over. Again, it may need a bit of watching and water to make sure it settles in well.

ALTERNATIVES: Lenten roses (*Helleborus orientalis* hybrids); hostas (*Hosta*) with big, strong green leaves; meadowsweet (*Filipendula palmata*)

Summer

Holdovers from Spring

» **'Rose Queen' barrenwort**
Epimedium grandiflorum 'Rose Queen'

The sweet diminutive leaves on this barrenwort were still looking fresh and adding a little green pocket in the underplanting, so we left her in.

New Plantings

» **Japanese fountain grass**
Hakonechloa macra 'Aurea'
WHAT IT IS: perennial grass
ZONES: 5–9
SWAP OUT: fall

This elegant Japanese native deserves a spot in every garden and perhaps every container. Its 12-inch-long, cascading leaves form a waterfall of gold. It prefers part shade but will grow well in sun, provided it has fertile soil and a good amount of moisture. It will grow to be a large (2–3 feet wide) mound in time but is a slow spreader. It was named the Perennial Plant of the Year in 2009 by the Perennial Plant Association.

INTO THE GARDEN: Japanese fountain grass could remain as a container plant and in the fall will show tints of pink and red (which it does in the garden, as well). We took ours out and planted it into the garden in a part-shade spot with lots of compost as mulch.

ALTERNATIVES: Japanese sedge (*Carex morrowii* 'Ice Dance' or 'Silver Sceptre'); *C.* 'Rekohu Sunrise'; *C. elata* 'Aurea'; hosta (*Hosta* 'Pot of Gold' or 'Prairie Moon')

» 'Hadspen Cream' bugloss

Brunnera macrophylla 'Hadspen Cream'

WHAT IT IS: perennial
ZONES: 3–7
SWAP OUT: fall

Do you ever wish you could have forget-me-nots but not have to remember to pull them up or to help them reseed? Do you ever wish that hostas had prettier flowers? Well, check out brunneras. They are lovely plants with several excellent cultivars that have gorgeous white-and-green-variegated leaves in different incarnations. And to top it off, in spring they have sprays of blue flowers in almost the same size and shape as those of forget-me-nots. Delightful! They grow well in shade and part shade and are adaptable to most soils. *Brunnera* 'Hadspen Cream' has leaves with a deep cream edge surrounding a center of green.

INTO THE GARDEN: The leaves are elegant enough that we planted them for that alone in our summer underplanting; however, you might find that the variegated bugloss varieties get a bit tatty by summer's end,

whether in the garden or in the container. So we moved them out into the garden and kept them well watered through the end of the autumn. You might find that next year you can plant them into the container in the spring and leave them in through two seasons.

ALTERNATIVES: *Brunnera macrophylla* 'Jack Frost' or 'Looking Glass'; variegated leopard plant (*Farfugium japonicum* 'Variegatum'); hostas (*Hosta* 'Patriot' or 'Francee')

» 'Quicksilver' foamflower

Tiarella 'Quicksilver'

WHAT IT IS: perennial
ZONES: 3–8
SWAP OUT: fall

A delicate, low-growing (to 15 inches) plant, this native American woodlander seems quite happy to be contained and is certainly very happy when located in a shady spot with moist, rich soil. Many excellent cultivars with gorgeous leaves and flowers have come on to the market lately. They make a fantastic substitute for heucheras (*Heuchera*) when you're looking for something slightly more delicate and refined.

INTO THE GARDEN: Like the bugloss (*Brunnera*), they could also be used in the container from the earliest days of spring until the dog days of summer. When planted into the garden, take care to give them lots of water in the early weeks of planting. Once the cooler days of autumn arrive, they can usually take care of themselves.

ALTERNATIVES: Heuchera (*Heuchera* 'Quilter's Scroll'), foamflower (*Tiarella cordifoliai*), false nettle (*Boehmeria* 'Hoksune-Mushi'), piggy-back plant (*Tolmiea menziesii* 'Taff's Gold'), beesia (*Beesia deltaphylla*)

» Crested lady fern

Athyrium filix-femina 'Vernoniae'

WHAT IT IS: fern
ZONES: 4–9
SWAP OUT: fall

Elegant as any fern out there, the crested lady fern is unique in that its smallest frond division (the *pinnule*) is divided again, giving the tips of the fern an exotic and fingerlike appearance. This variety is smaller than the regular species but just as lovely. Like many ferns, these

WOODLAND SHRUBBERY
PLANT PALETTES

graceful little beauties prefer moist soil in part or full shade.

INTO THE GARDEN: We find these ferns need to get out into the garden by late summer. They either start to look dreary or simply melt away with the summer heat. Either way, we dig them out and plant them into the garden in a suitable spot. They come back, sometimes taking a few years to get to a good size after having spent a bit of time living *la vida loca* in the container.

ALTERNATIVES: Lady fern (*Athyrium filix-femina, A.* 'Branford Beauty'), maidenhair fern (*Adiantum pedantum*), fall fern (*Dryopteris erythrosora*)

Fall

Holdovers from Summer

» 'Rose Queen'
barrenwort
Epimedium grandiflorum 'Rose Queen'

She stays calm and carries on. Really, she keeps plugging away with her sweet, crisp little green leaves. End of autumn is the perfect time to plant epimediums out into the garden. Plant, water, and let them be unless a dry spell hits; then keep them well watered.

New Plantings

» Bowman's root
Gillenia trifoliata
WHAT IT IS: perennial
ZONES: 5–9
SWAP OUT: winter

The popularity of this underrated super-deluxity is on the rise. At maturity in the garden, Bowman's root can grow to 4 feet and is covered in small, starry white blossoms. A total late-spring delight — excellent specimens often look like a cloud of tiny butterflies — and then it takes a bit of a rest before turning all shades of red, yellow, or orange in the fall . . . which stay for weeks before turning in for the winter. It's best for part shade or high, dappled shade and moist, rich soil.

INTO THE GARDEN: We left this brilliant baby in place until it was completely done flaunting its red goodness. And then we moved it out into the garden, into a border that was part shade, part sun. We're hoping for blooms this spring, but maybe we'll have to wait another year.

ALTERNATIVES: Barren strawberry (*Fragaria* 'Pink Panda'), creeping raspberry (*Rubus calycinoides*), eastern teaberry (*Gaultheria procumbens*), bunchberry (*Cornus canadensis*), hardy geranium (*Geranium sanguineum*)

» Pennsylvania sedge
Carex pensylvanica
WHAT IT IS: perennial sedge
ZONES: 4–8
SWAP OUT: winter

This small (8–10 inches tall) sedge is not often grown in specimen form, although it is delightful in this container in its casual, floppy kind of way. We think it should be grown more often both in containers and in the garden, where it grows most happily in shady, damp spots.

INTO THE GARDEN: If this container was to become a woodland bird haven for the winter months, the sedge could be left in to turn completely golden yellow and then tawny brown in winter, but we wanted to move it out into the garden.

We chose to place it down near a vernal pool — not quite on the edge but about 3 feet higher than the flood zone, underneath limbed-up pin oaks. Just perfect.

ALTERNATIVES: Fiber optic grass (*Isolepsis cernua*), corkscrew rush (*Juncus effusus* f. *spiralis*), Appalachian sedge (*Carex × appalachica*), weeping brown sedge (*Carex flagellifera*)

Winter

New Plantings

» ## Leucothoe
Leucothoe fontanesiana 'Rainbow'
WHAT IT IS: shrub
ZONES: 5–8
SWAP OUT: spring

Red, yellow, copper, and cream variegated leaves dazzle the arching branches of this super-fun eastern native shrub. This plant is great in the container or in a garden. After a jaunt in the container, try it out in the garden — it looks great when planted in combination with deciduous azaleas and early-blooming trees.

INTO THE GARDEN: This variety is well adapted to New England and seashore conditions. It prefers moist, well-drained, acidic soils. It's an excellent choice for a broad-leaved ground cover under larger trees and shrubs.

ALTERNATIVES: Creeping cotoneaster (*Cotoneaster adpressus* 'Tom Thumb') or rockspray cotoneaster (*Cotoneaster horizontalis* 'Hessi'), plum yew (*Cephalotaxus harringtonii*)

» ## Dwarf Siberian spruce
Picea omorika 'Nana'
WHAT IT IS: conifer
ZONES: 4–8
SWAP OUT: spring

Compact, dense, and globe-shaped when young, its shape gets more pyramidal as it ages. This spruce has great bicolor tendencies and is an excellent focal point in any under-story planting or container underplanting.

INTO THE GARDEN: Plant out into any neutral to acid well-drained bed in sun to part shade.

ALTERNATIVES: Japanese pieris (*Pieris japonica* 'Scarlet O'Hara'), Japanese holly (*Ilex crentata* 'Hetzii'), false holly (*Osmanthus heterophyllus* 'Goshiki')

» ## Boxwood
Buxus sempervirens 'Suffruticosa'
WHAT IT IS: evergreen shrub
ZONES: 5–9
SWAP OUT: spring

This classic selection is the gold standard when it comes to hedging. It grows slowly and holds any shape you want to impose on it. Left to its own devices, it will form a sweet, tidy globe.

INTO THE GARDEN: Plant out into the border or transfer to a smaller vessel and use it as a staple element. You can never have too many boxwoods.

ALTERNATIVES: False cypress (*Chamaecyparis obtusa* 'Kosteri'), cryptomeria (*Cryptomeria japonica* 'Mignone'), mugo pine (*Pinus mugo* 'Valley Cushion'), Japanese holly (*Ilex crenata* 'Helleri')

ADORNMENTS: Cut branches of staghorn sumac (*Rhus typhina*) with seed heads

Flowering Tree

FLOWERING TREES are the ultimate container plants! They are multidimensional: in addition to flowers, many of them offer great branch structure, textural bark, and interesting foliage. Sometimes you even get the bonus of fruit or berries. The dynamic nature of these trees is not the only appeal; they also tend to be readily available in small sizes at most nurseries. In small-scale landscapes, flowering trees in containers are incredibly valuable; they're often used to frame a doorway or to create a focal point.

Ideally, you should choose a tree whose mature height is less than 25 feet. There is also a benefit to selecting slower-growing trees: these have slower-growing root systems that will use up less space in the containerized setting, meaning they'll be happy in the vessel for a longer period.

Though we usually associate flowering trees with spring (think magnolia and cherry), flowers come at all different times of the year. The summer bloomers can be some of the most magnificent — for warm-climate gardeners, there are the long-lasting candy-colored blooms of the crape myrtle (*Lagerstroemia indica*). The early-summer display of sourwood (*Oxydendrum arboreum*) features clusters of sweet lily-of-the-valley blossoms, while stewartia (*Stewartia pseudocamellia*) displays camellia-like white blossoms among its magical zigzag branches. And nothing says fall magic better than the pure white peony-looking blossom of the franklinia tree (*Franklinia alatamaha*) hovering among fire-toned, almond-shaped leaves.

FLOWERING TREE
Spring

This is the magnolia's time to shine. Sweetly scented flowers hover above a charming display of light-toned pastels. With the weather warmer and the frost at bay, we decided to bring out some of our houseplants' babies. Over the winter we had identified which plants we would like to propagate for spring planting — in our case, ivy (*Hedera helix*) and piggyback plant (*Tolmiea menziesii* 'Taff's Gold'). After a few days of hardening off, they were ready to go into our planting. The fern shoots were uprooted from Roanne's yard, nursed in a recycled plant container overnight, and effortlessly transitioned into the planting. Just look how festive these fern crosiers look dancing around the stems of the magnolia, ducking in an out of tufts of grape hyacinth (*Muscari*) and patches of pansies (*Viola*). It just makes you want to dance around a maypole!

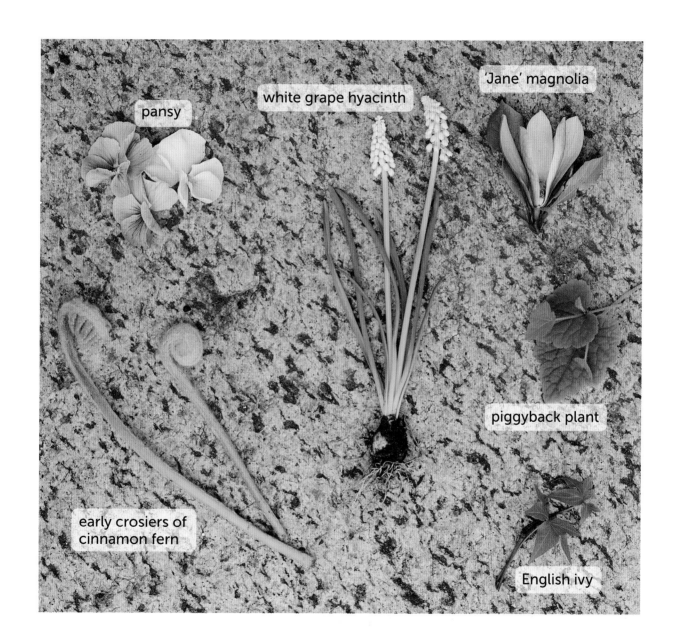

pansy

white grape hyacinth

'Jane' magnolia

piggyback plant

early crosiers of
cinnamon fern

English ivy

English ivy

'Pink Grapefruit' achillea

fairy rose

'Venus' heuchera

FLOWERING TREE
Summer

Magnolia's flowering had concluded and now we had a vessel full to the brim with healthy, shiny foliage. The homeowners enjoyed the soft pink palette and were thinking of adding some carpetlike roses into their garden. Why not try them in the container first? The vessel had plenty of room and depth to support the rose's crown. Both the ivy and the piggyback plant were doing very well at this point. We decided to keep the ivy (for its trailing habit), add some roses, try achillea (*Achillea* 'Pink Grapefruit'), and finish with a nice silvery heuchera (*Heuchera*). The piggyback plant reprised its previous role as a houseplant.

FLOWERING TREE
Fall

To create a fall feel for this planting, we used a combination of perennial divisions from the garden and natural decorations. *Sedum* 'Angelina' and *Coreopsis* 'Zagreb' needed a temporary home until their new bed in the garden was established, so we popped them in with the magnolia. The Saint-John's-wort (*Hypericum* 'Baby Lion') was a new cultivar we wanted to test, and this seemed like a good way to do it. Adding natural materials such as glycerine-preserved leaves, tiny gourds, and angel vine is a great way to spruce up a planting for a holiday, event, or after an unfortunate container incident (like forgetting to water while you were away on a weekend beach retreat).

Saint-John's-wort

glycerine-preserved leaves

'Angelina' sedum

'Zagreb' coreopsis

gourd

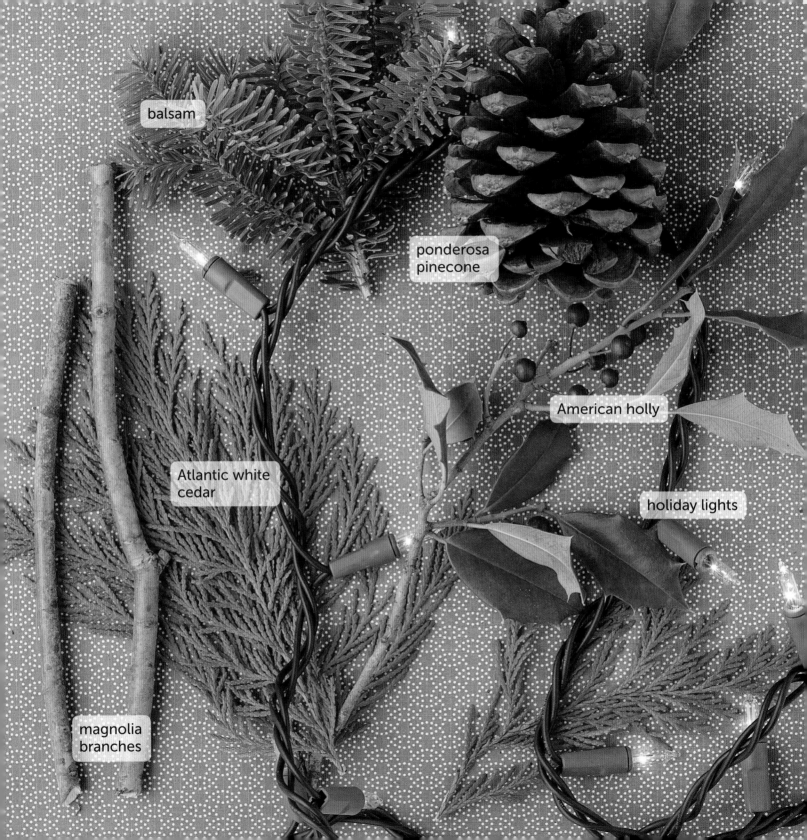

balsam

ponderosa pinecone

American holly

Atlantic white cedar

holiday lights

magnolia branches

FLOWERING TREE
Winter

It's wonderful to come home to sparkling white lights on a cold, dark winter afternoon. Lighting small ornamental trees is an art in itself. Be sure to keep to the natural lines and be gentle . . . especially when working with trees, like magnolia, that set next year's flowers early! Beneath these glowing branches is the simplest, most classic underplanting treatment there is — an arrangement of cut greens, berries, and pinecones.

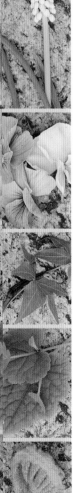

FLOWERING TREE
PLANT PALETTES

INTO THE GARDEN: Pot up tender varieties and bring them indoors for the winter; they make great houseplants. You can also select hardy varieties to plant as a ground cover later on, but be wary — this plant is invasive in many regions. Before planting into the garden, where it may wreak havoc, check one of the many invasive-plant watch-lists that exist online (see Resources, page 258).

ALTERNATIVES: Periwinkle (*Vinca minor* 'Alba'), moss phlox (*Phlox subulata* 'Snowflake'), wireplant (*Muehlenbeckia complexa*)

» Piggyback plant
Tolmiea menziesii
WHAT IT IS: tender perennial
ZONES: 7–9
SWAP OUT: summer

Little plantlets seem to just materialize at the base of the cute hairy, heart-shaped leaf. A plantlet appears to hover just above the leaf and to dance in the breeze, giving some motion to our planting. In Zones 8 and above, piggyback plant grows best in woodland conditions in moist soil. It is easy to propagate: just remove a mature leaf and leave in moist soil. We keep piggyback plant indoors for the winter and propagate it in a blend of 1 part rich potting soil and 1 part orchid moss. Fun fact: *Tolmiea* is closely related to our much loved foamflower (*Tiarella*).

INTO THE GARDEN: Leave outside until fall and bring in for the winter.

ALTERNATIVES: Foamflower (*Tiarella*), dead nettle (*Lamium maculatum*), heuchera (*Heuchera* 'Quilter's Joy'), bergenia (*Bergenia cordifolia*), lady's mantle (*Alchemilla mollis*)

» Early crosiers of cinnamon fern
Osmunda cinnamomea
WHAT IT IS: fern
ZONES: 4–8
SWAP OUT: summer

We chose this plant for its whimsical spirit, festive height, and soft texture. This lovely native fern is rather exquisite in three out of the four seasons. In the early spring it is almost impossible not to reach out and touch the soft, fuzzy, tawny-colored crosiers as they unfurl. These earliest fronds go on to become the bright cinnamon-colored fertile fronds of the plant. The more recognizable green sterile fronds emerge a bit later. In autumn, the plant turns a reddish brown–deep golden color. This fern prefers moist soil and shade and is often found in damp, marshy woodlands.

INTO THE GARDEN: We took ours out and transplanted them to a nook in Sara's shady garden. After planting, be sure to keep your ferns well watered until the snow flies. They may not look great this first year but should settle in fine by next spring.

ALTERNATIVES: Fritillaria (*Fritillaria imperialis*), Iceland poppy (*Papaver nudicaule*), cut stems of winterhazel (*Corylopsis pauciflora*)

Summer

» **English ivy**
Hedera helix

Ivy continues here as a pleasant texture spilling over the edges of the container. It's a lovely green foil to the sweetness of the rest of the container.

New Plantings

» **Fairy rose**
Rosa 'The Fairy'
WHAT IT IS: shrub rose
ZONES: 5–9
SWAP OUT: fall

This plant fits perfectly into our cottage farmhouse scene. The plant is fairly compact, a nice spreader with a bloom time from June until frost. Bloom power! Profuse clusters of double-petaled flowers dapple the base of the planting. This variety is relatively fragrance-free, which in my opinion is always a downer. Deadheading the spent blooms and removing dropped foliage is a must. Roses like good air circulation, and because it is in a packed container setting, we need to stay on top of her grooming, so as not to encourage disease.

INTO THE GARDEN: After we take out our plants in the fall, we transplant the rose, as is, into a new home in the garden. 'The Fairy' works well in many settings, from the cottage garden as a soft showy edge plant to an interesting ground cover surrounding beautifully shaped boxwood in the traditional garden. In the winter or early spring, we prune it back to 10 inches and reduce side shoots to three buds. If the plant is established and needs rejuvenation, cut down one out of every three stems to the base of the plant.

ALTERNATIVES: Shrubby cinquefoil (*Potentilla fruticosa* 'Pink Whisper'), weigela (*Weigela florida* 'Minuet'), bloody cranesbill (*Geranium sanguineum* 'Striatum'), garden phlox (*Phlox paniculata* 'Harlequin')

» **'Pink Grapefruit' achillea**
Achillea millefolium 'Pink Grapefruit'
WHAT IT IS: perennial
ZONES: 5–8
SWAP OUT: fall

We selected 'Pink Grapefruit' for her superwoman-like qualities; she is tough as nails. The bubble-gum flowers appear in a domed mass, which gives the planting a burst of color. When the initial fireworks have passed, the blossoms gently fade to a soft, dusty pink tone that pairs nicely with the silver foliage of the heuchera (*Heuchera*). The foliage is compact and that of resembles carrot or dill — lacy and fernlike with a silver shimmer. In the garden, achillea has a reputation for being unruly and messy. We wanted to explore how she would work in a crowded container setting. We found that she performed well and minded her manners. This particular New England summer was wet, so it was a bit tricky to balance watering and air circulation. In the end, her herby smell and chaotic habit of darting in and out of the underplantings made her a worthy companion.

INTO THE GARDEN: Achillea transplants best in the fall. Cut back the plant by as much as one-third to minimize its water loss. Transplant it in among other tough perennials, for *Achillea millefolium* has a tendency to be quite aggressive. Plant in full sun and avoid moist, über-fertile soil. Deadhead and

FLOWERING TREE
PLANT PALETTES

» 'Angelina' sedum

Sedum rupestre 'Angelina'

WHAT IT IS: perennial ground cover
ZONES: 3–11
SWAP OUT: winter

'Angelina' is always showy. Her sprucelike foliage holds color year-round, and ranges from a pure chartreuse to a golden yellow in spring and summer, then shifts to a burnt orange tone in the winter months. Her yellow flowers appear on occasion but are not missed if they don't show up. 'Angelina' will creep and trail out of the vessel, though she seems to creep with substance; she doesn't just send skinny legs down the side of the pot.

INTO THE GARDEN: 'Angelina' prefers to be planted in full sun in well-drained soil. She'll tolerate most soil types and is drought resistant. 'Angelina' transplants well, so break her into pieces and share the love.

ALTERNATIVES: Irish moss (*Sagina subulata*), club moss (*Selaginella kraussiana*), golden creeping Jenny (*Lysimachia nummularia* 'Aurea'), golden thyme (*Thymus vulgaris* 'Aureus')

Winter

An easy way to create an arrangement of cut greens around the rim of a container is to start with a standard evergreen wreath and add your own adornments. We call this the "wreath cheat," and it is our standby, time-saving holiday adornment go-to!

To begin, choose a wreath that is roughly the same size as the rim of your container but allows about an inch of greenery to extend beyond the rim (it's better to go too small than too big). Cut a slit in the wreath so it will slide easily over the base of the planting. To do this, cut the greenery with a pair of pruners, then use wire cutters to cut the wreath frame.

Slip the wreath around the base of the planting and run your hands around the wreath, fluffing the greenery upward. Use this wreath as a base, much in the way you'd use a frog or oasis foam in a flower arrangement. Stick cut mixed greens and other materials into the wreath, "beefing" up the base of the planting with additional colors and textures.

The brutal winter winds will eventually crisp out your underplanting. It is safe to say that lights and wreath should be removed in February. Cleanup is easy as the wreath just slips off. Take care when removing lights; you wouldn't want to sacrifice any spring flowers!

INSIDER TIP: Add fun trailing elements like clusters of incense cedar (*Calocedrus*) and seeded eucalyptus (*Eucalyptus*) by placing them underneath the wreath frame. Soften the look by placing more of the material (eucalyptus or cedar) into the wreath just above where you tucked it underneath, so it doesn't look as though it is a dangling afterthought.

Materials

Premade evergreen wreath with a diameter that when lying flat around the base of the container fits nicely with about 1 inch of greenery overlapping the edge of the vessel. (*Hint:* It's better to go too small than too big.)
Pruners
Wire cutters
Precut holiday greens
Additional ornamentation (picked pomegranates, pinecones, gilded fruit)

Cut Greens We Love

THERE ARE MANY GREENS AVAILABLE in the winter marketplace and many greens available in your own backyard. Some of our favorites are arborvitae (*Thuja*), Port Orford cedar (*Chamaecyparis lawsoniana*), incense cedar (*Calocedrus*), white pine (*Pinus strobus*), leucothoe (*Leucothoe*), pieris (*Pieris*), juniper (*Juniperus*), and shore pine (*Pinus contorta*).

If you're lucky enough to have access to a great floral shop, you may be able to get some super-luxe Dutch greens or festive West Coast beauties. We especially love the unusual cedars and cryptomerias that appear at the marketplace just in time to dress up your holiday container arrangements. Try a variety of different textures and colors. Have fun!

Very Berried

BERRIES and other colorful fruits have long been utilized in ornamental gardens to add color and interest to a cold, drab landscape. The palette of berries is almost endless, from the bright crimson fruits of 'Winter Red' winterberry (*Ilex verticillata* 'Winter Red'), to the golden tones of 'Lanzam' apple (*Malus domestica* 'Lanzam'), to the true purple of beautyberry (*Callicarpa dichotoma*). The container garden is a great place to get acquainted with different berry-bearing plants (say that 10 times fast) before they go out into the landscape.

A lot of berries taste great, too, of course, to humans and animals alike. And many that are not edible for humans are an excellent source of food for birds and other wildlife, helping to fuel them at a time of year when they most need the calories. Because of this, including these berried plants will attract more and varied birds to your garden. Like many gardeners these days, we've chosen to blur the lines between ornamental and edible gardens and use a dynamic container that is both tasteful and tasty.

In this arrangement, flowers, herbs, and foliage plants all mix together to form a tapestry of color, textures, and tastes surrounding the hero of our story, the highbush blueberry (*Vaccinium corymbosum*).

Now, here's a shrub for all seasons! In spring, he has sweet, white bell-shaped flowers. In summer we get to eat those delicious berries and in fall we enjoy his blazing foliage. Here's a berry-bearing shrub we're likely to plant wherever we go.

VERY BERRIED
Spring

At this stage, our blueberry is just a little bundle of potential. Its small, bell-shaped flowers and fun branch coloration are on display. Our plant is basically the same height as the vessel, which you'd think would run the risk of creating visual monotony; but here the unexpected pairing of wild plant and stylized container gives us the interest we need. In upcoming months, the blueberry will grow and the scale difference between the shrub and the container will increase, adding even more visual interest. A few edibles tucked around the base of the plant offer good snacking opportunities until the berries are ripe.

'Lolla Rossa' lettuce

blueberry

'Red Oak Leaf' lettuce

meadowsweet

thyme

curly parsley

'Kewensis'
wintercreeper

blueberry

blueberry

blueberry

Greek
oregano

'Hidcote'
lavender

lemon
verbena

curly parsley

VERY BERRIED
Summer

Blueberries are ready for snacking! Anytime someone goes out to pick blueberries, Paso, the dog, stands on his hind legs and joins in. Our blueberry has grown, and our planting takes on a casual, summer feeling. It's too hot for the lettuces (and they've mostly been eaten, anyway). The parsley is looking great; it has been harvested often, so its shape is quite nice. We thought it was good to have herbs so close to the kitchen, so we added some more. This time we put in some festive summer favorites: lemon verbena (*Aloysia triphylla*), oregano, and lavender. In the kitchen, lavender and verbena pair nicely with blueberries. The lemon verbena makes a great infusion for simple syrup and is a tasty way to sweeten summer berries.

VERY BERRIED
Fall

This combination reads like notes from a wine tasting: inky red, almost violet; bright garnet at the edge. Attractive textures, red plums, and a taste of aged leather. Colors consistent, tart plums, and subtle earth, a hint of red clay, nicely built on tart acidity and soft but substantial tannins. Fares well with a light cozy porch in a modern terra-cotta pot.

'Kewensis' wintercreeper

eastern teaberry

aster

showy oregano

blueberry

eucalyptus

privet berries

dwarf Alberta
spruce

bay leaves

VERY BERRIED
Winter

After we planted our blueberry out into the garden, we decided to dress up the container for the holidays. It wouldn't be winter in an American garden center without good ol' Alberta spruce. We thought we could dress it up a bit by placing it on the porch in our stylish little terracotta number. Remember: Your container is your cardigan, and tonight Alberta is changing out of her whiskeybarrel muumuu and going out in one of those glittery J.Crew cashmere cardigans that both Michelle Obama and Sara love.

We rimmed this planting with some natural silver-toned greens that we purchased at the flower market. Tucking seeded eucalyptus, euphorbia pods, privet berries, and bay leaves into the soil softens the edge of the vessel and makes Alberta sparkle.

VERY BERRIED
PLANT PALETTES

Spring
New Plantings

» **'Lolla Rossa' and 'Red Oak Leaf' lettuces**
Lactuca sativa 'Lolla Rossa' and 'Red Oak Leaf'
WHAT IT IS: leafy vegetable
ZONES: n/a
SWAP OUT: summer

Early lettuces have such a lovely texture. They come in a variety of colors ranging from the truest spring green to deep purple. In the container they pair nicely with bulbs or herbs, plus we always have some left over from planting in the garden, and we might as well put them to use.

INTO THE GARDEN: Pick, rinse, and toss with olive oil, salt, and pepper — *finito!*

ALTERNATIVES: Garden sage (*Salvia officinalis*), bugleweed (*Ajuga* 'Caitlins Giant'), arugula (*Eruca vesicaria sativa*), dandelion (*Taraxacum officinale*), baby broccoli (*Brassica oleracea italica*), mustard greens (*Brassica juncea*), sorrel (*Rumex acetosa*)

» **Curly parsley**
Petroselinum crispum
WHAT IT IS: biennial herb
ZONE: 7
SWAP OUT: fall

Parsley is an easy herb to find and to use. It's relatively cold tolerant and serves as a nice companion plant in the vegetable garden. Parsley attracts predatory insects, which attack pests and can protect crops like tomatoes. Its dense ripples give movement to the composition and its wiry stems seem to just pop out here and there, weaving in and out of the lettuce. Fun!

INTO THE GARDEN: Plant into a windowsill pot or into the herb garden for the remainder of the season.

ALTERNATIVES: Cilantro (*Coriandrum sativum*), Genovese basil (*Ocimum basilicum*), catmint (*Nepeta*), sweet marjoram (*Origanum majorana*)

» **Thyme**
Thymus
WHAT IT IS: herb
ZONES: 3–9
SWAP OUT: summer

Here's to our little trailer! The small, dappled texture of the thyme contrasts with the hefty lettuce leaves. It is sweet smelling and a standard addition to our scrambled eggs. Thymes come in a variety of shapes and sizes, fragrances, textures, habits, and flower and foliage colorations.

INTO THE GARDEN: Plant into a walkway, edge the herb garden, or let it creep along a stone wall. Plant thyme in a small vessel and add it to the potager. Container plant extraordinaire, small-scale ground cover, some are even evergreen — here's to thyme!

ALTERNATIVES: There are many thymes to play with: woolly (*Thymus pseudolanuginosis*) is nice, 'Elfin' is tiny, 'Latvian Lucy' is apple green, 'Goldstream' is gold flecked and lemon scented, and Mongolian thyme (*Thymus ibukiensis*) has the showiest pink floral display.

» **Meadowsweet**
Filipendula palmata
WHAT IT IS: perennial
ZONES: 3–9
SWAP OUT: summer

Showy clusters of flowers float above haired, raspberry-like foliage. We liked its texture and thought it would look nice skirting the blueberry for

Highbush blueberry

BLUEBERRY SPEAKS QUIETLY, so plant it in a setting where you can interact with it frequently to hear its whole story. Roanne and her family often visit the untouched shoreline of a New Hampshire lake, and every day she's there, she walks along paths that have her interacting with gorgeous blueberries. Some stand alone, while others mix with magical sweet fern (*Comptonia peregrina*), coastal sweetpepper bush (*Clethra alnifolia*), and bayberry (*Myrica pensylvanica*). No matter what season it is, she stops to take in the natural beauty of this plant.

For the best crop of berries, always buy an established plant from a reputable garden center, and be sure to ask if it will set fruit in its first year. There are many different cultivars of blueberry: early-fruiting, late-fruiting, small-berried, large-berried, plants with a compact habit (best for container planting), and those that grow taller (probably better for the garden). Many blueberries self-pollinate, but others need a mate nearby to produce fruit. A bit of research, then, before you go shopping will be helpful.

Once your blueberry leaves its vessel, plant it in full sun to part shade in moist, acid soil that is rich in organic matter. If you're planting many blueberry shrubs, to start a formal picking patch, space them at least 4 feet apart. Blueberries also look great in an informal woodland border. Early spring is the best time to prune away damaged or unproductive wood.

Zones: 3–7

Site analysis: This is a well-lived-in and fabulously comfortable home along the Slocum River in Massachusetts. Off in the distance, native blueberry and grasses grace its banks. The container planting is located on the porch outside the great room and kitchen, next to a screened-in portion, where the homeowner entertains. She's a marvelous cook, and we thought she would want to experiment with a variety of herb underplantings in spring and summer.

Best containers: Stylish, aged terra-cotta is classic yet fun; wooden cube vessels are vineyard chic; galvanized can be rustic yet modern.

Our container choice: We chose terra-cotta because we liked how its dusty patina played off the mahogany tones of the bark and the reddish purple tones of the blueberry's fall foliage display. The shape of this vessel also appealed to us — there was something fun about planting a native, free-flowing shrub in a stylized vessel. Also, we knew that the container wouldn't be staying outdoors for the vigorous thaw-and-freeze cycle that is January through March in New England, so we figured it would be okay to use terra-cotta. We planted the blueberry out into the garden in the fall and used the vessel for a holiday planting that would stay outdoors just through December and then be brought indoors.

Alternative plants: Blueberry is our favorite edible shrub. For ornamental shrubs, try beautyberries (*Callicarpa*), winterberry (*Ilex verticillata*), viburnums (*Viburnum*), *Photinia serratifolia*, skimmia (*Skimmia japonica*), red chokeberry (*Aronia arbutifolia*). Use berrying trees for a larger display — *Cornus mas* and *Malus sargentii* are great choices.

VERY BERRIED
PLANT PALETTES

Summer

spring. By summer it will be too tall and will be happier in the garden. Plant in full sun to part shade in rich, moist but well-drained soil.

INTO THE GARDEN: Cut the leaves to the ground if they become shabby or tattered, then await healthy new growth. Divide in fall or spring. It looks great planted in clusters behind big patches of astilbe.

ALTERNATIVES: *Rubus pentalobus* 'Emerald Carpet', strawberry (*Fragaria vesca* 'Yellow Wonder' or 'Mignonette'), lowbush blueberry (*Vaccinium angustifolium*)

Holdover from Spring

» **Parsley**
Petroselinum crispum

Parsley will stay trim and tidy and continue to produce shoots as long as you keep picking it. Once it goes to flower, though, its flavor is less desirable and bitter.

New Plantings

» **'Hidcote' lavender**
Lavandula 'Hidcote'
WHAT IT IS: perennial herb
ZONES: 5–8
SWAP OUT: fall

'Hidcote' is a dwarf variety of common lavender that is said to have the truest lavender fragrance. The flower is very purple and has almost a navy blue tint to it. Lavender's spikes of narrow silver leaves give a shimmer to the base of the planting, complementing the subtler sage green colorations.

INTO THE GARDEN: Lavender does well in the garden, especially in warm, dry climates. Tuck it into a mixed border among some roses or plant it in mounded rows for harvest-

ing. Lavenders like well-drained soils that lean toward the sand-gravelly side. Once established, lavender thrives on neglect. Prune it by one-third a few weeks before the killing frost and mulch it with straw.

Another option for cold, wet climates is to overwinter lavender plants in individual terra-cotta pots. We harvest all the lavender foliage we need for the winter, wrap the container in burlap, and tuck it in close to the house, on the southwestern side. We like the idea of bringing lavender indoors for the winter, but practically speaking, it just doesn't work well. A very bright window may be able to offer enough sunlight, but the reality is that most houses are kept too warm and lavender needs some time to chill. All in all, it's happier outside.

ALTERNATIVES: Curry (*Murraya koenigii*), rosemary (*Rosmarinus*), feverfew (*Tanacetum parthenium*), basil (*Ocimum basilicum*), chocolate mint (*Mentha piperata*)

» Lemon verbena
Aloysia triphylla

WHAT IT IS: herb
ZONES: 9–10
SWAP OUT: fall

Lemon verbena is beloved for its out-of-this-world fragrance. It may be the perfect lemon smell — not too sour, not too sweet. The long, pointy, true green leaves grow on woody stems and can be harvested at any time. If you're not aggressively snipping leaves, unassuming white flowers will appear. The great thing about this plant is its ability to thrive. For every stem you cut, three will appear in its place. Dried leaves retain their fragrance and can be used in oil infusions. Trim evenly to maintain a compact shape or let it grow wild to add motion to your planting.

INTO THE GARDEN: Lemon verbena is not the prettiest plant to overwinter indoors — it will lose its leaves and go dormant for about three months. Give it a good haircut and keep it from drying out completely, and it will repay you with tasty new leaves in the spring. Once the danger of frost has passed, you can place it outside in the pot or transition it into the garden.

ALTERNATIVES: Pineapple mint (*Mentha suaveolens*), thyme (*Thymus*), savory (*Satureja hortensis*), tricolored garden sage (*Salvia officinalis* 'Tricolor')

» Greek oregano
Origanum heracleoticum

WHAT IT IS: herb
ZONES: 5–9
SWAP OUT: fall

The oregano family is diverse. It includes oreganos that are Greek, Sicilian, Italian, Syrian, Cretan, Kyrgystani, and Mexican. All are part of the genus *Origanum*. Cuban oregano, which is a *Plectranthus*, is the true beauty. Its gorgeous, furry, succulent foliage has a beautiful sea green sheen. Some say she's edible, which is hard to believe since she carries a pungent smell reminiscent of Soft Scrub. Whatever your taste preferences may be, the oregano family has a great visual presence and cute trailing habit in the container.

Greek oregano is the real deal. Its flavor is so intense that when eaten straight off the stem, it numbs your tongue. Don't confuse it with our invasive friend *O. vulgaris* (wild marjoram), which is almost tasteless. Taste and flower color are the best indicators of variety. Greek = intense flavor/white flower; wild marjoram = weak flavor/pink flower.

INTO THE GARDEN: Plant it into the garden as a maintenance-free ground cover and harvest when needed. If you don't get around to cutting it, spiky flower stalks of white will appear. Like most herbs, oregano tastes best when harvested before it flowers.

ALTERNATIVES: Ornamental oregano (*Origanum* 'Kent Beauty'), creeping raspberry (*Rubus calycinoides*), creeping rosemary (*Rosmarinus officinalis* 'Prostratus')

» 'Kewensis' wintercreeper
Euonymus fortunei 'Kewensis'

WHAT IT IS: perennial ground cover
ZONES: 5–9
SWAP OUT: winter

We like the look of *Euonymus* 'Kewensis' creeping up our trees. Its tiny little evergreen

201

Twelve Containers through the Year

Transplant Time

IT'S HARD TO PICTURE a garden without sun-loving perennials. They're the main characters of the cottage garden, the essence of the formal border. Sun-loving perennials have a lot to offer the gardener — a huge palette with endless amounts of color, texture, and flower power. And they have the need to be dug up and divided every so often, so if you're growing them in a garden, you've got a ready supply of container planting candidates!

For this planting, in fact, we wanted to see what it would be like to fill a container entirely with garden transplants. We love the idea of using transplants; for one thing, they're free! Often, they're plants that would be either tossed into the compost or thrust upon every visitor who comes to the garden. Also, plant-lovers that we are, we like to see common plants, which may feel ordinary in the garden, elevated to rockstar status in containers, where their individual characteristics can be highlighted.

The classic shape of this fluted, cast-stone container can accommodate a lot of looks, which is helpful for our purpose of using transplants from the garden. We like this vessel because it works well with both short, round plantings and tall, wispy ones. We sited the container on a beautiful back terrace overlooking Warrens Point in Little Compton, Rhode Island. These plants have all come from the surrounding property, so they're somewhat used to the windy and salty air. The garden here is immaculate. The idea of transitioning plants in and out of the garden is exciting, and inspires us to pull out more planters and adorn the pool in a similar manner.

TRANSPLANT TIME
Spring

The spring we planted this container, the lady's mantle (*Alchemilla mollis*) was growing like crazy and self-sowed into the pea-stone path. *Voilà!* Instant container candidates, with very little work and no cost. The lady's mantle offered a lovely bright green and chartreuse color story, so we paired it with some true blues; we had some leftover grape hyacinth bulbs that we forced for another project, so we added these to the composition. Dividing the cushion spurge in Roanne's garden was on her to-do list, so we added some to bring forth a bit more chartreuse until the lady's mantle flowered. The last element in the planting was veronica, which wasn't a transplant but rather a leftover from another container planting. The color story was sweet and festive; we especially loved how the grape hyacinth danced in and out of the vessel.

veronica

grape hyacinth

lady's mantle

cushion spurge

'Blue Glitter' sea holly

Frikart's aster

'Chocolate' joe-pye weed

'Blue Hobbit' sea holly

plumbago

lady's mantle

TRANSPLANT TIME
Summer

This season we wanted to try working with sea holly (*Eryngium*) in a container-ized setting, so we divided some 'Blue Glitter' sea holly to see how it would do. We liked the compact scale of the spring planting but also wanted to test some taller, leggier perennials, such as Frikart's aster (*Aster × frikartii*) and 'Chocolate' joe-pye weed (*Eupatorium* 'Chocolate'). Would the underplantings give these plants the support they need? Do they hold up well enough to serve as "staple" plant? (In the end, the answer was "Yes!") We decided to keep the lady's mantle in for another sea-son; its foliage was holding up well and would tidy up the rim of the planting alongside the plumbago.

TRANSPLANT TIME
Fall

The fall container took on a golden olive hue. The once deep purple–brown leaves of the joe-pye weed turned and the mini-marshmallow blooms lingered on. We loved the deep violet legs of the plant, and enjoyed its last hurrah before cutting it back. As we wanted the planting to still have a rich burgundy element after joe-pye was swapped out, we searched the garden for a dark volunteer and found a hefty clump of heuchera, which looked a little lost in a big island driveway planting. Then we transplanted some snow-in-summer (*Cerastium tomentosum*) from another container planting that was being dismantled.

'Quilter's Joy'
heuchera

'Emerald Blue'
moss phlox

'Chocolate'
joe-pye weed

snow-in-summer

Pennsylvania
sedge

pinecone

pomegranate

lotus pod

so that it is more than halfway inserted in the foam base. Set the staked form into the soil-filled container to make sure it fits properly — the stake should be touching the bottom of the vessel and the base of the form should be resting on the container's edge.

Once you know the staked form will fit, take it out of the vessel and work with it lying flat on a table or other work surface. For our arrangement, we alternated pomegranates and pinecones in bands circling the foam cone form and filled the spaces in between each pomegranate and pinecone with a little cluster of nesting material (you could also use Spanish moss or reindeer moss). The pomegranates and pinecones were attached to the foam using small wire-wrapped stakes. Using floral glue, we affixed the mini pinecones (golden or natural) in the gaps between the pinecones and nesting material.

After the arrangement was dry, we placed it back on the stake and secured it with a drop of hot glue. Once the hot glue was dry, we inserted the staked form into the container. Lovely!

Wire-wrapped stakes make it easy to create arrangements with pinecones, lotus pods, and pomegranates.

Ornamental Grass

ORNAMENTAL grasses add variety to both gardens and container plantings. Not only do they offer interesting texture, cool variegation, and different heights, but they also bring movement and sound to the garden experience. Grasses can blend into the landscape; they effortlessly look as though they've been there forever. The same grass that has delicately and inconspicuously graced the back corner of your garden for years can look remarkably different when enshrined in frost or when adorned with dew droplets that sparkle in the morning light. They can give a gentle type of structure to the garden, with soft lines and blurred edges.

For every soft-flowing, gentle grass such as *Pennisetum* 'Little Bunny' or Mexican feather grass (*Nassella*), however, there is a sharp, aggressive, bladed one. Grasslike plants such as phormium (*Phormium*) and acorus (*Acorus*), and fescues (*Festuca*), can add a sharp slash or a spiky relief to the planting. Stylistically, grasses are as flexible as their individual blades. One kind of grass planted en masse in a single container can evoke a casual, beachy feel or a crisp, modern one, depending on the style of the container.

Planted as a mix of grasses, using a variety of tall and short plants, fat and thin blades, plain green and variegated, you can make your container or garden feel like you've arrived in some kind of lovely, exotic prairie. Grasses of all types (in fact, even those that are not true grasses, such as lilyturf [*Liriope*] and dwarf mondo grass [*Ophiopogon*]) are excellent when used in a mixed container, like the kind we plant here. They easily mix and mingle with a wide variety of other plants — perennials, shrubs, and trees.

ORNAMENTAL GRASS
Spring

Grasses are often slow to emerge in the spring, but we still wanted to evoke the essence of grass — long, slender blades; verticality; and motion — so we added chives for the grassy presence they contributed to this planting of hens-and-chicks (*Sempervivum*). (Another idea is to leave out the chives and have a total hen-and-chick party.) The planting also offers a lot of contrast, between the delicate green blades of the chives and the kaleidoscope of colors found in the dense, circular form of the hens-and-chicks. These are most colorful in spring, and are actually hardier than you might think by looking at them. We also added *Sedum* 'Dragon's Blood', with its succulent ruby-edged leaves draping over the edge of the container, to provide a visual resting place.

chives

hens-and-chicks

'Dragon's Blood' sedum

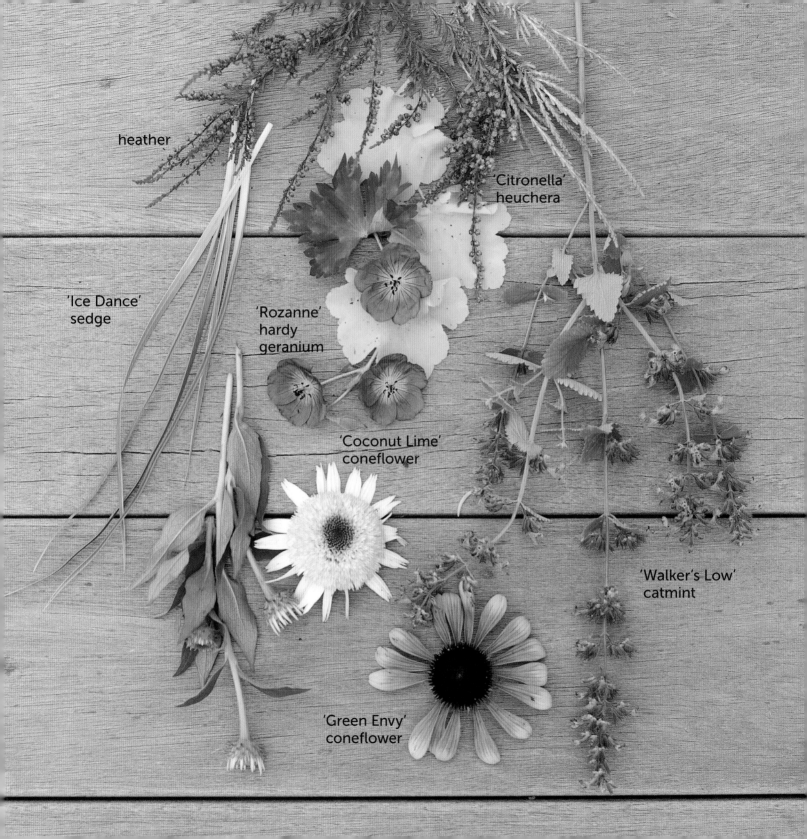

heather

'Citronella' heuchera

'Ice Dance' sedge

'Rozanne' hardy geranium

'Coconut Lime' coneflower

'Walker's Low' catmint

'Green Envy' coneflower

ORNAMENTAL GRASS
Summer

We could have kept our big yummy bowl of hens-and-chicks and chives intact all summer long, but we decided to dismantle the container and naturalize the collection of hens-and-chicks among some woolly and lemon thymes. We also wanted to experiment with more grasses, to test some combinations for a garden we were designing. We needed to try out plants that didn't mind being close to the sea, and wanted to use perennials that had a relaxed, meadowy, cottage feel to them.

ORNAMENTAL GRASS
Fall

For the fall, we knew we wanted to play with some yellow and rust-toned switchgrass (*Panicum*) we saw glistening in a quiet corner of the nursery. Its golden twinkle drew us in, and then BAM . . . we walked by a pot of bluestar (*Amsonia*) and it knocked our socks off. The feathery golden stems blew in the wind like the hair of an '80s supermodel. Paired in the container with a mix of collaborators from the delicate and sweet boltonia to crunchy Swiss chard, you have an ensemble that can withstand the test of time.

'Heavy Metal' switchgrass

bluestar

golden Swiss chard

'Ice Dance' sedge

'Snowbank' boltonia

creeping Jenny

variegated
boxwood

'Ice Dance'
sedge

juniper

dwarf Alberta
spruce

holly

'Heavy Metal'
switchgrass

false
cypress

ORNAMENTAL GRASS
Winter

We love the visual imagery of grasses encrusted in the frost; whether short or tall, the icy blades create motion, even though they're frozen and unmoving. We wanted to use the Alberta spruce (*Picea glauca* 'Conica') in a more naturalized setting, so you could see that when paired with other shrubs and grasses, Alberta can evoke a more relaxed seasonal feeling. 'Ice Dance' sedge has been in the composition for three seasons now — what a flexible container plant! Variegated boxwood brings a nice splash of color to the foreground, and the dark shiny leaves of holly nicely play off the wild passages created by the grasses. Cut juniper, holly, and false cypress (*Chamaecyperis*) fill in the gaps between grass and spruce.

ORNAMENTAL GRASS PLANT PALETTES

Spring

New Plantings

» Chives

Allium schoenoprasum

WHAT IT IS: perennial herb
ZONES: 3–9
SWAP OUT: summer

This tasty little number is a delicate grasslike plant; it actually resembles lawn grass. Chives seem very tame, even though they're not (to prevent seeding, cut off faded flowers). They don't grow very tall (about a foot) and have very ornamental (not to mention edible!) lilac-colored flowers. Chives are happy in a pot outdoors or on a windowsill, as long as they have lots of sun and even moisture.

INTO THE GARDEN: You can use this little herb in so many ways: plant it into your herb garden or in a pot by the door, harvest the tops for an omelet, and plant the bulbs in your garden for the ornamental flowers. If you keep chives in the container, cut them back several times during the growing season to maintain their health and vigor — and to eat!

ALTERNATIVES: Corkscrew rush (*Juncus effusus*), lilyturf (*Liriope muscari*), sea thrift (*Armeria maritima*), chamomile (*Anthemis nobilis*)

Container Close-Up

WE CHOSE THIS LARGE ROUND concrete bowl because we were drawn to its striking ratio of width to height — it is wider than it is tall. While the bowl mimics the horizontal nature of the house and deck, the height of the grasses and tall, slender perennials offer a striking counterpoint. The wide bowl gives us a lot of room to experiment with perennial textures, and its semicircle form just begs to be filled. This gives us an opportunity to experiment with different grasslike plants in each season.

The container rests on a deck that overlooks the water, a site with a sense of openness and uncluttered modernity. The nearby vegetation is made up of native grasses, shrub roses, and sumacs that offer a grounding backdrop to each season. The deck, which doesn't have a railing, is essentially an extension of the living room when the doors are open during the summer. In addition to being a decorative element, the vessel plays a role in keeping visitors safe: it marks the edge of the deck.

» Hens-and-chicks
Sempervivum

WHAT IT IS: perennial
ZONES: 3–9
SWAP OUT: summer

Looking very tropical, ground-hugging hens-and-chicks are durable and happy to be planted in tight, big groups, provided they have sharp drainage and sun. Hens-and-chicks can be found in a wide range of colors (chartreuse, true green, burgundy, ruby red, terra-cotta, lilac-blushed), textures (tubular leaves, cobwebbed, multitoned, fuzzy, smooth), and sizes (tiny to large). We don't look forward to seeing this plant flower: the plant matures, sends up a spike-like flower stalk, and then the mother hen dies, leaving her orphaned chicks behind.

INTO THE GARDEN: Hens-and-chicks are best appreciated in mass plantings. As we moved into subsequent seasons, it would show up as one here and one there, so taking them out is the best option. From this container, individual rosettes could be planted into their own little terra-cotta pots, moved into your gravel walkway, or nestled next to a tea light or at

All About Grasses

THE TERM *ORNAMENTAL* GRASS can be a little tricky because many plants fall under that umbrella: the true grasses (Gramineae family), the sedges (Cyperaceae family), the rushes (Juncaceae family), and even hardy bamboos (from the genus *Phyllostachys*). Phormiums are sometimes thrown into the mix as well. While classification of ornamental grasses may be a bit complex, taking care of them isn't. Grasses are extremely adaptable and tolerate a variety of soil mediums. In some cases, a good ol' crew cut at the end of the growing season is all they need. Grasses can be utilized in a variety of settings and can be great garden problem-solvers. Some of them are good ground covers in poor soils, tall ones serve well as a natural screen, and others can be planted along an embankment to control erosion.

Many common varieties of ornamental grass are imported from other regions. Maiden grasses (*Miscanthus*) are Asian introductions; they're known for their delicate, cascading, waterfall-like foliage and their silky flower tassels that linger into the winter. Feather reed grass (*Calamagrostis acutiflora* 'Karl Foerster') has a wheatlike look that makes it one of the most festive and most recognizable grasses. Switchgrass (*Panicum virgatum*) is an American native whose blade tips turn burgundy in the fall.

Most grasses grow best in four to six hours of sun. When planted in too much shade, blades may get floppy. The coloration of grasses planted in shade may fade, too. Every genus of grasslike plant requires a different amount of water, because even though they all have the same grassy look and are often referred to as grasses, many of them are botanically very different from one another. For example, switchgrass can thrive in drier conditions than a sedge can; mondo grass can practically grow in standing water. Watering is a big variable, so read your plant labels well.

ORNAMENTAL GRASS
PLANT PALETTES

the bottom of a napkin during a dinner party. Or you could stick a bamboo skewer into a rosette and insert it into a floral arrangement. If you plant hens-and-chicks in the garden, give them a spot with good drainage.

ALTERNATIVES: Sedum (*Sedum makinoi* or *S. album*), club moss (*Selaginella kraussiana*), Irish moss (*Sagina subulata*), pansy (*Viola*), peppermint (*Mentha × piperita*)

» **'Dragon's Blood' sedum**
Sedum spurium 'Dragon's Blood'

WHAT IT IS: perennial
ZONES: 4–9
SWAP OUT: summer

This selection comes from a great genus of plants that range in shape, color, texture, and form. 'Dragon's Blood' has red-edged, succulent leaves that are scalloped at the tops. The stems are ropey and root easily from each leaf node. Tough and durable, it requires sharp drainage and sun; otherwise it becomes kind of rangy and loses its color.

INTO THE GARDEN: Once this stonecrop has done its job in the spring container, it is best planted out into the garden. We took out this one when we changed over to summer, planting it straight into the garden, where it has thrived. It did so well, we almost put it back in for fall, which could have been a lovely addition had we chosen a slightly different color palette.

ALTERNATIVES: Sedum (*Sedum* 'Angelina'), mazus (*Mazus reptans*), wintercreeper (*Euonymus fortunei* 'Kewensis'), fiber optic grass (*Isolepsis cernua*), curly onion (*Allium senescens* var. *glauca*)

Summer

New Plantings

» **'Ice Dance' sedge**
Carex 'Ice Dance'

WHAT IT IS: ornamental grass
ZONES: 5–9
SWAP OUT: spring

This plant looks kind of like a beefier lilyturf (*Liriope*). It's much denser and can grow up to 12 inches tall. Like most carexes, 'Ice Dance' prefers full to part shade and moderately moist soil. We found that it did extremely well in the container, tolerating much more sun than we had expected. Its stiff blades have a deep, dark green center and crisp, ghost-white edges. It's fun to see how a low-growing, grasslike plant can take a dominant role in our container planting. Even though at this distance the plant basically reads as green, it commands the composition with its explosive motion. It cascades just enough to soften both the edge of the bowl and some of the legs of the coneflower (*Echinacea*).

INTO THE GARDEN: You can plant the sedge in a more shaded area if you'd like. Its markings stand out well among hostas, gingers, and other woodland ground covers. In the winter, cut to the ground and apply a light mulch. We have had good luck overwintering it in the container; just be sure to give it enough water come spring.

ALTERNATIVES: Lilyturf (*Liriope muscari*), Mexican feather grass (*Nasella tenuissima*), blue fescue (*Festuca glauca*), variegated rush (*Juncus variegata*)

» 'Green Envy' coneflower

Echinacea 'Green Envy'

WHAT IT IS: perennial
ZONES: 4–9
SWAP OUT: fall

A very unusual echinacea! As the lime green flowers of 'Green Envy' mature, the petals take on a magenta streaking. The flower elongates from its rounded shape, and the cone takes on a deep purple hue. Like most coneflowers, this plant can tolerate heat and periods of drought once established, and will max out in height at around 3 feet.

INTO THE GARDEN: Plant into the garden and enjoy its beautiful coloration. Echinacea makes great long-lasting cut flowers, both when the flowers have petals and when they're just conelike pods. Mix them with classic purple coneflower (*Echinacea purpurea*) or plant them among some *Nicotiana* 'Lime Green' and 'Hot Chocolate'.

ALTERNATIVES: *Zinnia* 'Green Envy', *Nicotiana* 'Lime Green'

» 'Coconut Lime' coneflower

Echinacea 'Coconut Lime'

WHAT IT IS: perennial
ZONES: 4–9
SWAP OUT: fall

Another festive and unusual echinacea. White petals surround a pom-pom of chartreuse florets — the visual equivalent of a poodle or maybe a fancy jellyfish. Enjoy the whimsical showcase of flowers from June until frost!

INTO THE GARDEN: Plant in the garden, in a place where they can be noticed — they are too showy to hide. Plant a patchwork of coneflower varieties and marvel at the range of colors and all the butterfly visitors.

ALTERNATIVE: *Echinacea* 'White Swan'

» 'Rozanne' hardy geranium

Geranium 'Rozanne'

WHAT IT IS: perennial
ZONES: 5–8
SWAP OUT: fall

Who can resist a deep purple-blue color? Its flower is pure and wonderful, and its color is a pleasure to have in the garden. Large, saucer-shaped flowers appear May through September. This plant is tough: heat tolerant and a vigorous grower. In the container, it will trail and swirl in and out of the underplanting. In the garden, the semi-marbled foliage will mound up and fill any spot its heart desires. In fall, the leaves take on a nice mahogany tone.

INTO THE GARDEN: Plant in the garden in partial shade for best results. We like to plant this one among *Brachyglottis greyii* and globe thistle (*Echinops ritro*).

ALTERNATIVES: Canterbury bells (*Campanula lactiflora*), balloon flower (*Platycodon grandiflorus*), soapwort (*Saponaria officinalis*), scabiosa (*Scabiosa caucasica*), knautia (*Knautia macedonica*)

» Heather

Calluna vulgaris 'CW Nix' and 'Minima Smith V'

WHAT IT IS: woody subshrub
ZONES: 4–9
SWAP OUT: fall

We enjoy using heaths and heathers in our container plantings year-round. Roanne first fell in love with them while working at Sylvan Nursery, a great nursery that specializes

ORNAMENTAL GRASS
PLANT PALETTES

in heath and heather propagation (check out its website in Resources, page 258). 'Minima Smith V' has a little floral display of tiny pink flowers that appear from August to September, with the real highlight being the bright green foliage. In winter, it turns a beautiful rust-red, making it a colorful addition to a winter conifer collection. It has an erect dwarf habit that works nicely in a variety of container combinations. 'CW Nix' has a profuse amount of plum-purple flowers that bloom from August to October. The flowers really stand out against its deep green foliage.

INTO THE GARDEN: Plant in a hole at least twice the diameter of the root ball. Fill the hole with compost and do not plant too deeply, for both heath and heathers have shallow root systems. Plant in full sun to partial shade; in shade their colors become less vibrant and the plants tend to get a little leggy. Never let them dry out, as underwatering is the leading cause of death among heathers, and dress them with buckwheat mulch.

ALTERNATIVES: Lilyturf (*Liriope muscari*), angelonia (*Angelonia angustifolia*), lavender (*Lavandula* 'Hidcote'), germander (*Teucrium chamaedrys*)

» 'Citronella' heuchera
Heuchera 'Citronella'
WHAT IT IS: perennial
ZONES: 4–8
SWAP OUT: fall

This pale chartreuse, small-leaved heuchera looks a lot like the selection 'Lime Rickey' but is a bit paler. Try not to bake this fellow, for he will melt.

INTO THE GARDEN: We always try to move this into the garden, and we always end up with a struggling plant, so this fits into the category of "perennials that behave like annuals." We still love it, though, so we'll keep trying to find a happy home in our gardens for it.

ALTERNATIVES: Sedum (*Sedum* 'Angelina'), lady's mantle (*Alchemilla mollis*), lemon-scented geranium (*Pelargonium citronellum*)

» 'Walker's Low' catmint
Nepeta 'Walker's Low'
WHAT IT IS: perennial
ZONES: 3–10
SWAP OUT: fall

Catmints are prolific bloomers and their fragrant gray-green foliage looks great in the border. In Ro's parents' garden, the plants are always flat in the middle because one of the cats — Mia, Sophie, or Ralphie — is always curled up asleep inside them. This variety blooms all summer and never gets leggy, staying a nice compact size of 1 to 3 feet tall by 1 to 3 feet wide. It can tolerate partial shade and is not only for kitties — the bees and hummingbird moths love it, too. Catmints have done really well in our containers; it's nice to see such a staple perennial thrive in the contained setting.

INTO THE GARDEN: Go with a classic combination and plant with daylilies (*Hemerocallis*) and *Sedum* 'Autumn Joy' in the garden. Plant in well-drained soil. In midsummer cut it down by a half, and in two to three weeks it will be blooming again. It's super hardy, both in and out of the container.

ALTERNATIVES: *Verbena bonariensis* 'Souza', *Salvia* 'May Night', giant hyssop (*Agastache* 'Blue Fortune'), blazing star (*Liatris spicata*)

Fall

» 'Ice Dance' sedge
Carex 'Ice Dance'

'Ice Dance' looked so great in the container, we had to leave him in for another season. It complements the switchgrass nicely: the sedge adds interest to the underplanting, while the switchgrass serves as a grounding element for the airy boltonia.

New Plantings

» 'Heavy Metal' switchgrass
Panicum 'Heavy Metal'
WHAT IT IS: ornamental grass
ZONES: 4–9
SWAP OUT: spring

Some of the switchgrasses can get leggy and unruly. Not 'Heavy Metal' — its foliage is more upright and a bit shorter, which allows it to work well clustered among other plants in a containerized setting. Its summer foliage is blue-green (which would also look great with the summer foliage of bluestar). It is adaptable to most soils and is slow to clump.

INTO THE GARDEN: The roots of switchgrass grow best in warm soil, so be sure to transplant during the late spring or early summer, just when you're about to sow beans or corn into the veggie garden. Plant too early in the spring or too late in the fall and roots may rot, killing the plant. We overwintered this swtichgrass in the vessel.

ALTERNATIVES: Miscanthus (*Miscanthus sinensis* 'Flamingo' or 'Morning Light'), switchgrass (*Panicum virgatum* 'Shenandoah' or 'Prairie Sky')

» Bluestar
Amsonia tabernaemontana
WHAT IT IS: perennial
ZONES: 5–9
SWAP OUT: winter

You would never guess that bluestar's bushy, willow-like foliage starts out a silvery blue-green color, kind of like eucalyptus. Native and quite rugged, this plant has a very sweet and unusual steel-blue flower. Plant in sun or part shade.

INTO THE GARDEN: Plant into the garden in sun or part shade. If you plant in the shade, you may want to cut back the plant by one-third after flowering to prevent an untidy fall show.

ALTERNATIVES: Fall fern (*Dryopteris erythrosora*), *Sedum* 'Autumn Joy', black-eyed Susan (*Rudbeckia* 'Goldsturm')

» 'Snowbank' boltonia
Boltonia asteroides 'Snowbank'
WHAT IT IS: perennial
ZONES: 4–9
SWAP OUT: winter

A fabulous late bloomer and a wonderful addition to any garden, boltonia sports lots of snow-white blooms in fall. We planted this combination once buds were set, but if you planted it earlier, you could cut back the plant by one-third in July to keep the blooms coming along through October.

INTO THE GARDEN: Plant in the garden anywhere you're looking for a frothy white display of late-blooming flowers. It naturalizes well and looks best when planted en masse. Divide in early spring.

ORNAMENTAL GRASS
PLANT PALETTES

ALTERNATIVES: Giant hyssop (*Agastache* 'Blue Fortune' or 'Black Adder'), Asian aster (*Kalimeris integrifolia*), coreopsis (*Coreopsis* 'Autumn Blush')

» ## Golden creeping Jenny
Lysimachia nummularia 'Aurea'
WHAT IT IS: perennial
ZONES: 4–9
SWAP OUT: winter

This is a prostrate creeping perennial ground cover that mats at about 2 feet tall and can tail to about 10 inches long. Its little chain droplets root easily at the joints. 'Aurea' is less vigorous than the standard version (that's a good thing, though).

INTO THE GARDEN: We don't bother planting creeping Jenny out in the fall; we just plant it in trays or recycled window box liners and cover with a heavy mulch for the winter. We find it a bit too aggressive in the garden, but love it in containers. Plants overwinter in plastic pots or trays quite nicely; give it a try! Be sure to keep them protected from strong sun, for their golden foliage will burn.

ALTERNATIVES: Greater periwinkle (*Vinca major* var. *variegata*), English ivy (*Hedera helix* 'Gold Heart'), mother of thyme (*Thymus serpyllum*)

» ## Golden Swiss chard
Beta vulgaris 'Golden Lights'
WHAT IT IS: vegetable
ZONES: n/a
SWAP OUT: winter

A fall ornamental staple, its deep crunchy leaves are adorned with golden yellow legs and veins. This variety is a nice true yellow; sometimes you're lucky and you'll get some creamy canary yellow stems mixed in. It's a welcome departure from the crimson version.

INTO THE GARDEN: Cut chard stems and use in your Thanksgiving centerpiece or add them to your feast. We like combining chard with roses of varying sizes. We find that they hold up best when utilized in a hand-tied bouquet, but they fare well when placed in oasis foam.

ALTERNATIVES: 'Niko' Chinese cabbage, 'Orange Fantasia' chard, 'Burlesque' endive, 'Dwarf Blue Curled Vates' kale (all readily available and easy to start from seed)

» ## Barren strawberry
Waldsteinia ternata
WHAT IT IS: perennial
ZONES: 4–9
SWAP OUT: winter

Barren strawberry is a lush evergreen ground cover. This plant is closely related to the strawberry and has small, hard, hairy fruit. It grows best in humus-rich soil in partial sun, though it will tolerate sun if it has enough moisture. We really like its nice berry-stained autumn color.

INTO THE GARDEN: Plant this evergreen, carpet-forming perennial in partial shade. Tiny yellow, strawberry-like flowers appear in early spring and look really sweet hovering above their glossy leaves. This plant will spread on its own, but if you want even more, propagate by division.

ALTERNATIVES: Bergenia (*Bergenia cordifolia*), variegated strawberry (*Fragaria vesca* 'Variegata'), creeping raspberry (*Rubus calycinoides*), false strawberry (*Duchesnea indica*)

Winter

Holdovers from Fall

» 'Ice Dance' sedge
Carex 'Ice Dance'

The wide, now taupe blades of this sedge are a wintry yet still fluid part of this composition. Their shape helps to keep this container visually consistent from season to season, regardless of their color. We overwintered 'Ice Dance' in the container. After the pale winter blades go tatty from the season's winds — usually around late February — we cut it all the way back and mulch it in for the season.

» 'Heavy Metal' switchgrass
Panicum virgatum 'Heavy Metal'

The sedge takes the low road; the switchgrass, the high road. We liked having two different grasses continue through into spring, or at least until they both looked ready to be cut back.

New Plantings

» Dwarf Alberta spruce
Picea glauca 'Conica'

WHAT IT IS: conifer
ZONES: 2–6
SWAP OUT: spring

Conical with tight needle formation — this is a standard garden center staple for winter.

INTO THE GARDEN: Plant out into the border with a collection of heaths, heathers, and assorted conifers.

» Variegated boxwood
Buxus sempervirens 'Marginata'

WHAT IT IS: shrub
ZONES: 5–8
INTO THE GARDEN: spring

Clad in leaves with irregular, creamy yellow margins against dark green centers, this is a great choice for adding a dash of color to the underplanting in winter. This is the only dwarf variegated boxwood that holds its creamy variegation in shaded conditions.

INTO THE GARDEN: Plant in well-drained soil in a location that will provide morning sun to filtered shade. This makes a great focal feature planted alongside other mini conifers, heath, and heather.

ALTERNATIVES: Other variegated finds: false cypress (*Chamaecyperis obtusa* 'Baldwin'), hemlock (*Tsuga canadensis* 'Gentsch White'), holly tea olive (*Osmanthus heterophyllus* 'Goshiki')

ADORNMENTS: Cut juniper sprigs, chamaecyparis, holly stems, and clean snow!

Structure & Vines

VINES HAVE the ability to enchant. Their spirit, vigor, and variety bring vibrant color, unusual flowers, and sometimes fragrance to the garden. Vines are also super functional. Plant ivy on a trellis to form a living screen, one that creates privacy, blocks out the wind, and absorbs sound. Grow wisteria on a pergola to create a space where you can retreat to the shade or have a new area for shade-loving perennials.

Experimenting with vines in a containerized setting is a great way to become acquainted with these clingy friends. Annual vines grow quickly, whereas the perennial varieties, like wisteria, grape, and trumpet vines, take years to establish and bloom and may look rather awkward when planted at the base of a dominating structure. Establish the vine in the container (as the beautiful staple element of your planting), then transplant a more massive plant at the base of your pergola. Some vines — like roses, clematis, hops, sweet pea, and honeysuckle — are best grown in an ornamental setting. These vines are smaller in habit and don't require years to get to a size at which they can be appreciated. They will be happy growing on whatever beautiful plant support you can find.

Ornamental structures look great supporting flowering vines or left bare as a landscaping accent. Twig trellises add a touch of garden whimsy, while metal structures with ornate finials add elegant vertical interest. Tepee, trellis, obelisk, pyramid, rod, and stake: these essential garden props are beautifully functional. Can you say that about Mr. Garden Gnome? Okay, maybe yours wards off slugs or magically deadheads your petunias or brings your life a sense of purpose, but the fact remains that most acts of garden adornment do not translate into anything functional.

STRUCTURE & VINES
Spring

We knew we wanted to have a structure for this planting, and we knew that for spring we really couldn't choose anything other than sweet pea, with her frilly pink flowers and curly tendrils and big fat blue-green leaves. We used the color of the sweet pea's blooms and leaves as our jumping-off point for the whole composition. The planting has a charming silver sheen to it — lamb's ear (*Stachys byzantina* 'Helen von Stein') gives soft texture and weight to the container, while rosemary lends a finer textural balance and a piney scent. Woodland phlox brings the cheery pink down to the crown of the planting.

'Oranges and Lemons' blanketflower

'Dolce Peach Melba' heuchera

rosemary

'Goldflame' honeysuckle

lamb's ear

STRUCTURE & VINES
Summer

What we loved most about our spring planting was the fragrance of the sweet pea and the cool, blue-green leaves of the woodland phlox. For the summer planting, we chose 'Goldflame' honeysuckle not only because it's fragrant, but also because its leaves are reminiscent of woodland plox. The lamb's ear still looked fabulous, so we kept it in for another season. We liked how the rosemary skirted in and around the lamb's ear, so we left it in, too.

To amp up the planting for summer, we chose the daisylike 'Oranges and Lemons' blanketflower. To complete our planting, we added 'Dolce Peach Melba' heuchera, another tough-as-nails plant that contributes a gentle silvery orange shimmer on one side and a carmine-violet underbelly.

STRUCTURE & VINES
Fall

When fall arrived, our container was still blooming nicely but we were ready for change. We wanted to overwinter the honeysuckle in the container, so we gave it a massive haircut and let it spend the fall in a diminished state at the base of the vessel. To keep with the structural theme of the planting, we chose an ornate gathering of curly willow to be our central element. We rimmed the vessel with an assortment of rich, jewel-toned, crunchy ornamental veggies and the fall standard, the ornamental mum (*Chrysanthemum* × *grandiflorum*). Cold tolerant and festive, mums lend themselves to the autumn harvest theme.

'Bull's Blood' beet

'Cardinal' Swiss chard

purple sage

'Plum Pudding' heuchera

garden mum

ornamental kale

curly willow cluster

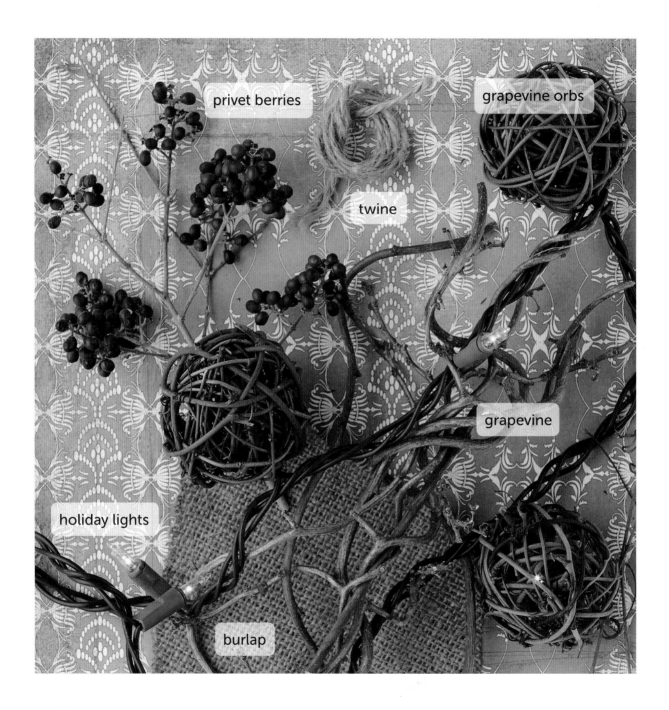

privet berries

twine

grapevine orbs

grapevine

holiday lights

burlap

STRUCTURE & VINES
Winter

It's nice to have some quick garden fixes in your holiday adornment repertoire. Here's an easy way to disguise a bare structure or a plant that needs protection. We wrapped our bamboo structure in burlap and dressed it up in lights, privet, and grapevine. You could easily use evergreen garlands like laurel and cedar, or even garlands of natural materials such as cranberries, pinecones, and chestnuts. Lights spruce up the composition and add sparkle to the texture of the burlap.

STRUCTURE & VINES
PLANT PALETTES

Spring

New Plantings

» **Sweet pea**
Lathyrus odoratus
WHAT IT IS: annual vine (tendrils)
ZONES: n/a
SWAP OUT: summer

Sweet peas are a classic cottage-garden plant. They will happily climb up any structure their tendrils can grasp on to. We bought this sweet pea already growing on the bamboo trellis, but we've started them before in little grow pots indoors and outdoors during late March or early April. There is nothing like the fragrance of a sweet pea.

INTO THE GARDEN: Take plants out and compost; be sure to cut all flowers for mini-bouquets before you do the deed. And don't forget to harvest seeds!

ALTERNATIVES: Hops (*Humulus lupulus*), *Clematis* 'Bee's Jubilee', English ivy (*Hedera helix*), five-leaf akebia (*Akebia quinata*)

» **Creeping phlox**
Phlox stolonifera 'Pink'
WHAT IT IS: perennial
ZONES: 3–7
SWAP OUT: summer

This mat-forming evergreen creeper with loose clusters of mildly fragrant flowers grows best in rich, moist soils. The

Starting Sweet Peas from Seed

GIVE YOUR SWEET PEAS a head start by sowing seeds in containers indoors during late winter and transplanting into larger container plantings as soon as the weather warms up. Sweet peas can tolerate light frosts, so they can be planted out a bit earlier than other seedlings.

You can start sweet peas in small containers (we like using little yogurt containers after poking drainage holes in the bottom), using a good potting mix with great drainage. Once the seeds germinate, they can be moved to a warm, sunny window. When the plants have three or four sets of leaves, move them to your larger outdoor container. Plant three to five of the baby sweet peas in a 24-inch-diameter vessel and place a bamboo or willow tepee in the container. Enjoy watching them grow and climb!

Get to Know Your Vines

PAIRING THE VINE OF YOUR DREAMS with the right trellis in the right container with the right conditions sounds tricky, eh? Get to know your vines and it's not as difficult as you think.

Vine can be classified into four categories, based on how they attach themselves to structures:

The twiners. These vines have flexible stems that wrap around their support. Some examples are wisteria (*Wisteria*), hyacinth bean (*Lablab purpurea*), honeysuckle (*Lonicera*), hops (*Humulus*), and annual morning glory (*Ipomoea*). Some perennial twiners, such as wisteria and five-leaved akebia (*Akebia quinata*), take years to establish and need strong support (like a wooden pergola). Annual varieties and smaller vines can climb up supports made of sturdy willow.

The root attachers. These vines grow small root-like holdfasts that adhere to a wall or structure. Such plants are a little harder to use on thin wire trellises but look great growing up a textured concrete wall or wooden fence. The English ivy (*Hedera helix*), Boston ivy (*Parthenocissus tricuspidata*), and some varieties of Virginia creeper (*Parthenocissus quinquefolia*) belong to this category.

The tendril climbers. This group of climbers is our favorite. They attach to their host by tendrils — little modified stems or leaves that reach out and twist around a structure. Sweet pea (*Lathyrus*), passionflower (*Passiflora*), and clematis (*Clematis*) belong to this grouping. Tendril climbers are the easiest to employ and look great climbing up a variety of structures.

The leaners. The last group of climbers needs a bit of help from us. The leaners have no built-in system for attachment, so they must be tied on. The best examples of leaners are climbing roses. Once the plant is tall enough, start attaching it to your trellis or wooden obelisk with twine or one of the other "attaching" products we mention in the Get a Grip sidebar (see page 251).

Vine success comes with proper pruning. Employ the proper pruning methodology at the right time of year and you will be rewarded with an abundance of blossoms. Pruning also encourages strong limbs and keeps the plant tidy. We don't want the plant to revert to a tangled mass of foliage now, do we? The best time to prune depends on when the vine flowers. Spring-flowering vines respond best if pruned after they finish flowering. Most other vines prefer to be pruned when they are dormant. Twining vines initiate growth from their upper buds, so without a yearly hard cutback the plant's lower sections will become straggly and leafless. Be sure to do some research and find out if your plant blooms on old wood, new wood, or both, so as not to cut off next year's display.

STRUCTURE & VINES
PLANT PALETTES

leaves have five flat, notched, petal-like lobes that appear at the stem tips in spring. These elliptical droplets dangle from the stem, giving motion to the planting. This is a woodland species that appears in fields and along streams. As the common name suggests, *Phlox stolonifera* spreads rapidly by stolons, forming little colonies of pink. Be sure to maintain the planting by removing damaged leaves and deadheading spent blossoms. The densely planted base of the container does not have the best air circulation, so keep a watchful eye out for powdery mildew.

INTO THE GARDEN: Plant out in the shade garden or keep in the vessel for the summer. If it is staying in the vessel, be sure to keep it mulched and moist. Plant *P. stolonifera* beneath woodland shrubs along with toad lily (*Tricyrtis*), wood anemone (*Anemone nemerosa*), and barrenworts (*Epimedium*).

ALTERNATIVES: Plumbago (*Ceratostigma plumbagnoides*), moss phlox (*Phlox subulata*), sweet woodruff (*Galium odoratum*)

» Lamb's ear
Stachys byzantina 'Helen von Stein'
WHAT IT IS: perennial
ZONES: 4–10 (requires more shade in warmer zones)
SWAP OUT: fall

Fuzzy, pale green, suedelike leaves form cute little mats in the garden or container setting. Lamb's ear is a perfect plant to use in the children's garden; its soft texture begs to be petted. Lamb's ear spreads rapidly in the garden, but in the container it is a little rock star. Divide plants from the garden and pop them right into your container combination. Lamb's ear is tough as nails! Ours grew so well, we even divided it a few times while it was growing in the vessel. Shifting it in and out and all around the vessel was no problem — we just provided some extra water and a little break before introducing new friends to the underplanting.

INTO THE GARDEN: In the ground, plants can get a little unruly, so it's best to plant out among other cottagey-feeling perennials and let them dance in and out and all around them. Plant with classics such as *Salvia nemorosa* 'May Night', Flower Carpet roses, lady's mantle (*Alchemilla mollis*), and purple coneflower (*Echinacea purpurea*)

ALTERNATIVES: Bergenia (*Bergenia cordifolia*), lady's mantle (*Alchemilla mollis*), common primrose (*Primula vulgaris*), snake's head fritillary (*Fritillaria meleagris*)

» Rosemary
Rosmarinus officinalis
WHAT IT IS: perennial
ZONES: 7–10
INTO THE HOUSE: fall

Rosemary is readily found in nurseries, garden centers, and grocery markets. We find that rosemary adds a nice subtle texture to the container planting. It's also really useful; we use it in the kitchen daily, so there can never be too much! When densely clustered amid other underplantings, rosemary can get a bit straggly. Keeping it trimmed will help it to stay looking fresh.

INTO THE GARDEN: Rosemary plant care is easy. Provide it with well-drained, sandy soil and at least 6 hours of sunlight and it will be happy indoors or out. Since rosemary can't withstand winters below 30°F, we like to keep it planted in a container so that we can easily bring it indoors at the end of fall. Rosemary prefers to remain on the dry side, so terra-cotta pots are a good choice. Visually, *we* prefer them — herbs look great in aged terra-cotta. Water thoroughly, then let rosemary dry out between waterings. We find that our rosemary blooms in winter when we bring it indoors. Its brilliant blue flowers look pretty nestled among the sticky evergreen needles. You could even try training your rosemary into a topiary.

ALTERNATIVES: Herbs such as curry plant (*Helichrysum angustifolium*), tarragon (*Artemisia dracunculus*), and lavender (*Lavandula* 'Hidcote')

Summer

Holdovers from Spring

» Rosemary
Rosmarinus officinalis

We liked the rigidity that rosemary gave this composition, in contrast with the floppiness of the honeysuckle and blanketflower, but mirrored the upright nature of the tripod.

Get a Grip

SOMETIMES YOUNG CLIMBING PLANTS need a bit of help getting started on their upward journey. Here are a few of the many different ways to attach your vine to its structure, to help it get a grip:

Nutscene garden twine. Classic, simple, tried and true. This British garden staple comes in cute tins and in a variety of colors. Works especially well with bamboo and willow trellises. Great for honeysuckle.

Velcro reusable plant ties. Strength and convenience all wrapped into one. No tying necessary, and incognito — they blend nicely into plants' foliage. Work especially well with metal caging (think tomatoes).

Soft ties. Rubbery outside, strong galvanized steel core. Gentle enough to tie together plants and strong enough to lash together supports. Works especially well when attaching a number of trellises for big climbing vines.

STRUCTURE & VINES
PLANT PALETTES

» Lamb's ear
Stachys byzantina

Soft, lovely lamb's ear helped keep the continuity from season to season. After a little trim in late spring, it came back as beautiful as ever.

New Plantings

» 'Goldflame' honeysuckle
Lonicera × heckrottii 'Goldflame'
WHAT IT IS: perennial vine (twining)
ZONES: 5–9
SWAP OUT: fall

'Goldflame' has candy-toned flowers that bring a summery feel to the planting. Its watermelon-colored, tubular buds open up to reveal creamy tangerine throats that give off a lovely fragrance that peaks in the evening hours. 'Goldflame' is also known as ever-blooming honeysuckle, as it blooms non-stop from mid- to late spring until fall. Hummingbirds and butterflies adore this plant as much as we do. In spring, 'Goldflame' sends up long, bendable canes from the center of the plant and can grow

to several feet in just a matter of days. Once they're exposed to sun, the canes become more rigid and lose their flexibility, making them much more difficult to train. During the summer and fall, continue pruning new cane shoots as well as any damaged, dead, or diseased branches. Do most of your pruning while the plant is dormant (in the case of our honeysuckle, in February). Remove any long, whippy growth to ground level. This will encourage your honeysuckle to sprout new growth at ground level, preventing bare stems or ones that are top-heavy with foliage. Prune to your heart's desire, although we suggest pruning from half to a third in order to preserve its existing shape; 'Goldflame' is a vigorous grower that blooms on new growth.

INTO THE GARDEN: Plant along a stone wall and let it do its magic, or plant in a bare spot of your garden, stake it down with irrigation ties, and train it as a ground cover. Just be sure to plant it somewhere where both you and the hummingbirds can enjoy the plant's many likable features.

ALTERNATIVES: Passionflower (*Passiflora incarnata*), snail vine (*Phaseolus caracalla*), Dutchman's pipe (*Aristolochia elegans*), clematis (*Clematis* 'Gravetye Beauty')

» Heuchera
Heuchera 'Dolce Peach Melba'
WHAT IT IS: perennial
ZONES: 4–9
SWAP OUT: fall

'Dolce Peach Melba' forms a compact clump and in the garden grows to about 8 inches tall by 16 inches wide. The foliage offers warm and inviting tones of peach, silver, and coppery red. The different hues change with the seasons and offer broad bursts of color to the composition. Heucheras are easy to use in the container, making them one of our favorite perennial underplantings.

INTO THE GARDEN: Plant heucheras out into the garden in fall. A good, healthy plant will be just as happy planted in the sun as it is in the shade. Bright morning sun with afternoon shade is the best balance. We find that established heucheras — ones that have been in the garden for three or four years — tend to push themselves up out of the soil. If this happens, dig up the plants, give them a trim, divide if you want, and replant into the ground or into the container. If you find they're shifting out of the ground in the winter due to the freezing and thawing of the ground, grab a handful of mulch or salt-marsh hay and insulate the crowns. Keep in mind that some of the new hybrids are not as vigorous as others. It's worth the investment to purchase a proven cultivar, and to select plants that are clearly healthy and well grown.

ALTERNATIVES: Heather (*Calluna* 'Firefly'), chameleon plant (*Houttuynia cordata* 'Chameleon'), shamrock (*Oxalis* 'Sunset Velvet'), coleus (*Solenostemon* 'Rustic')

» 'Oranges and Lemons' blanketflower

Gaillardia 'Oranges and Lemons'
WHAT IT IS: perennial
ZONES: 3–10
SWAP OUT: fall

Gaillardia 'Oranges and Lemons' is a flower-blooming powerhouse. The multitoned, orange-ringed cone is sur-rounded by daisylike, tangerine petals with gold tips. 'Oranges and Lemons' is a true pleaser — in addition to its blooms, it graciously withstands heat, humidity, poor soil, and even drought, once established in the garden. This blanketflower offers the container planting a fresh face and a bold swirl of sunset hues that unify the planting's color story.

INTO THE GARDEN: Transplant into the garden when you switch out your seasonal under-planting in the fall. Place in any bare trouble spot in a border that needs a bit of orange. The reliable blooms of 'Oranges and Lemons' will liven up any patch it graces. Deadheading will pro-long the bloom, although it's not critical to the plant's success. By midsummer, if there happens to be a lull in blossoms, cut it down to about 5 inches and wait for a glorious autumn show. 'Oranges and Lemons' maxes out around 20 inches high, so it's a perfect plant for the middle tier in the perennial border. Plant a patch of it in front of and among *Verbena bonariensis* or with any other fabulously pur-ple flower, such as giant hyssop

(*Agastache* 'Blue Fortune'), Russian sage (*Perovskia atriplic-ifolia*), or catmint (*Nepeta* 'Six Hills Giant').

ALTERNATIVES: Blanketflower (*Gaillardia* 'Fanfare'), coreopsis (*Coreopsis lanceolata*), golden marguerite (*Anthemis tinctoria*), black-eyed Susan (*Rudbeckia* 'Goldsturm'), osteospermum (*Osteospermum* 'Symphony Peach')

Fall

» Curly willow cluster

WHAT IT IS: ornamental sticks
ZONES: n/a
SWAP OUT: winter

A mahogany web of branches dances above a deep-toned assortment of ornamental veg-gies and herbs. The motion of the willow adds life to the base of the composition, which looks like a Dutch still life. In our opinion, it's not worth cul-tivating such an aggressive, messy plant. The best way to obtain these sticks in bulk is to purchase them from your local florist or garden center. They are generally sold in three

STRUCTURE & VINES
PLANT PALETTES

heights, in a range of tints, from yellow-amber to mahogany, and in bunches of 10. If you place them in the vessel, they may even root (just as do pussy willow and redtwig dogwood). We massed them in a central cluster and kept an eye on the cut-back honeysuckle, which gradually rejuvenated and made its way back up the willow branches. To cast a spooky glow on the planting, we nestled in a low-heat, staked spotlight. You can use a variety of colored bulbs from flickering orange to basic white. Be sure no dried debris is resting on a bulb, and to be super-safe, do not leave on overnight.

INTO THE GARDEN: Save for later use. Insert back into your vessel next fall or make a festive willow wigwam for the kids.

ALTERNATIVES: Other cut twigs such as birch (*Betula*), dogwood (*Cornus*, the orange Dutch varieties), and mossy sticks, or use black spray paint on found twigs from the yard. Roanne once used black-light paint on birch branches and gourds.

» 'Cardinal' Swiss chard
Beta vulgaris 'Cardinal'
WHAT IT IS: vegetable
ZONES: n/a
SWAP OUT: winter

This colorful variety of Swiss chard is extremely useful in and out of the container and garden. Its glossy green, ripple-textured leaves contrast with the long, vibrant red stems and veins. The base of the planting hosts a nice exchange between shiny and dull, with the chard's waxy leaves glistening amid the dull matte, purple-toned cabbage. Garden centers are starting to realize the mass appeal of ornamental fall crops like chard, and often stock nicely grown 4-inch pots that are ready for fall displays and container plantings. These plants are also easy to grow, so we recommend doing just that: start seeds indoors or sow directly into the ground; young seedlings transplant easily.

We love to use chard in seasonal containers and to fill gaps in the September garden (they look especially dreamy in front of all sorts of ornamental grasses). 'Cardinal', with a crimson-colored stem, is the most commonly grown variety. Try substituting 'Bright Lights' for a multitoned look. It comes in a medley of colors from oranges, to yellows, to brilliant reds and creamy whites.

INTO THE GARDEN: Plant extra seedlings in the garden or in 4-inch recycled plastic pots for later use—in other plantings, in floral arrangements, or just for eating. When sowing directly in the garden, one planting will last the entire year, so plan a permanent place for your chard rows to reap all its harvest.

ALTERNATIVES: Crunchy fall veggies such as 'Bright Lights' chard (*Beta vulgaris* 'Bright Lights'), tatsoi (*Brassica narinosa*), 'Redbor' kale (*Brassica oleracea*), and white and pink cabbages (*Brassica oleracea*)

» Purple sage
Salvia officinalis 'Purpurea'
WHAT IT IS: perennial
ZONES: 5–9
SWAP OUT: winter

The purple-toned leaves of sage gradually turn green as the plant matures, giving it a nice multidimensional look. Most people plant this variety as an ornamental, and though it's pretty, it's also pretty flavorful. This particular variety can grow up to 3 feet tall, but it naturally maintains a bushy appearance. Plant into the garden in sandy to rocky, well-drained soil in full to partial sun. We can't stress enough how visually adaptable this planting is; it's so great to have extras in 4-inch pots to employ in almost any composition anytime you have a textural hole at the base of your planting.

INTO THE GARDEN: Plant purple sage into the garden or into a nice big terra-cotta pot for the remainder of the fall season. Once, Roanne went to change out a client's planting on a chilly December morning and saw that the sage was looking great. The rest of the plants weren't looking so good, in the midst of the thaw-and-freeze cycle, so she chiseled the sage out of the frosty soil and planted it in pots that live in our kitchens.

ALTERNATIVES: Lamb's ear (*Stachys byzantina*), 'Icterina' garden sage (*Salvia officinalis* 'Icterina'), santolina (*Santolina chamaecyparissus*)

Dressing Up for Halloween

WE BOTH GARDEN WITH OUR CHILDREN, so we're always looking for fun ways to usher in the holidays without being tacky or relying on too many unnatural elements. This container planting seemed perfect for placing next to the front door to light the way for trick-or-treaters. The light makes the planting look like a crackling cauldron of fire! Nestle in some pumpkins, fresh from the patch, add a few crows, and you have a spooky Halloween vignette.

STRUCTURE & VINES
PLANT PALETTES

» 'Bull's Blood' beet
Beta vulgaris 'Bull's Blood'
WHAT IT IS: vegetable
ZONES: n/a
SWAP OUT: winter

Boasting delicate, deep red-burgundy-stained leaves that drape over thin stems, beets are a great addition to any fall container combination, for they add a dramatic dark spot of color and a cascading effect. The beet carries some of the same coloring as the chard, so they work well when paired together. The beet is much more delicate and uniform in color and doesn't have the vertical habit of the chard.

INTO THE GARDEN: Since it's so late in the year, we suggest that you harvest the plant and do a leaf taste test. If the leaves are tasty, add them to your salad mix or use them as a garnish. If they are too bitter and rough, either add them to the compost or feed them to the chickens. You can harvest the small beets — they're tastier when young. Cut them open and take a look at their cute candy-striped interiors. They also make a great natural dye.

» Cabbage and kale
Brassica oleracea
WHAT IT IS: vegetable
ZONES: n/a
SWAP OUT: winter

These are cold-tolerant fall staples that appear in every garden center alongside the parade of fall mums and cornstalks. Ornamental cabbages and kales are a great addition to your autumn container or mixed border. They offer a wide range of curly, crinkly, frilly leaves in a variety of colors, from pure white, to blue-silver, to pink and purple. There are so many varieties of differing heights and shapes — the combinations and uses are limitless.

The only problem with these new fall garden center staples is they do not come with instructions for tasteful design. With their very rigid stalks and large, circular shape, they can be difficult to incorporate with other plants. Roanne used to be quite scared of them until the first time she visited the Stonewall Kitchens flagship store and saw the work of our dear friend Jackie Nooney. Her combinations of amaranth (*Amaranthus*), orange-toned coleus (*Solenostemon*) and the magically tall and dark castor bean (*Ricinus communis*), and a big path of 'Redbor' kale (*Brassica oleracea*), inspired her and encouraged her to introduce ornamental veggies into some of her own combinations.

INTO THE GARDEN: Ornamental cabbage and kale colors intensify in cooler temperatures, so at the time the containers switch out, they'll still be looking great. If they haven't frozen, you can cut them and use them in a seasonal arrangement: Create a textural holiday centerpiece by intermixing cabbage or kale heads with amaranth (*Amaranthus*), rose hips (*Rosa*), boxwood (*Buxus*), coneflower pods, and other textures from the garden. If you want to jazz it up a bit, it's just as easy as a trip to the grocery store. Seckel pears, persimmons, mini eggplants, and chestnuts can be spiked on wooden picks and added to your arrangement.

ALTERNATIVES: Lettuce (*Lactuca sativa*), mini pumpkins (*Cucurbita*), euphorbia (*Euphorbia* 'Diamond Frost')

» Garden mum
Chrysanthemum × *grandiflorum*
WHAT IT IS: perennial, often sold as an annual
ZONES: 5–8
SWAP OUT: winter

This is a reliable fall crop and garden center staple — you can find mums in all sizes, colors, and textures. We like to display mums in a couple of ways. One is to place a large, bushel-sized mum in a round vessel with creeping rosemary cascading down the side and a nice big hefty grouping of curly willow nestled in the center. Another is to employ them as an accent to seasonal veggies. When we use mums in these plantings, we stick to monotone combinations so the floral display of the mums is subtle.

INTO THE GARDEN: If you dig up a mum early enough, you may have some luck transplanting it into the ground before it freezes. We've both had some

fantastic self-sown volunteers overwinter in the garden and enjoyed a decent second-year showing.

ALTERNATIVES: Pansies (*Viola*), aster (*Aster novi-belgii*), black-eyed Susan (*Rudbeckia* 'Goldsturm')

» 'Plum Pudding' heuchera
Heuchera 'Plum Pudding'
WHAT IT IS: perennial
ZONES: 4–9
SWAP OUT: winter

'Plum Pudding' is another of our favorite purple heucheras. It's similar to 'Palace Purple', but has a fine, silvery network pattern on its foliage.

INTO THE GARDEN: Plant where it will receive morning sun and afternoon shade in moderately moist, well-drained soil.

ALTERNATIVES: Heuchera (*Heuchera* 'Obsidian'), chameleon plant (*Houttuynia cordata* 'Chameleon')

Winter

To create this holiday arrangement, we started by swaddling our bamboo tepee with burlap

and wrapped it with ornamental red jute twine (you could also pin or staple it). We added the finishing touch by winding strings of holiday lights with fresh grapevine boughs — an homage to the vine! — around the structure. The ends of the grapevine can be secured in the soil or pinned to the burlap seams. We adorned the base of the planting with grapevine orbs and privet-berried boughs and topped it off with a hand-crafted grapevine star.

INSIDER TIP: You can also use this treatment for a practical yet stylish way to wrap up boxwoods and other plants in windy locations. After applying a late-fall dose of Wilt-Pruf or other antidesiccant, wrap up precious shrubs with burlap and adorn them with lights and vines. Get the kids involved and use fun-colored jutes, birdseed ornaments, and popcorn-and-cranberry garlands. Or use old cookie molds and make ice ornaments. Roanne's daughter, Nora, goes to her grandmother's house to make icy alphabet letters encrusted with hemlock pinecones and berries.

RESOURCES

Blogs and Websites That Inspire Us

Colorgirl
www.colorgirlalyn.blogspot.com

Design Sponge
www.designspongeonline.com

Gardens Illustrated
www.gardensillustrated.com

MarthaStewart.com
www.marthastewart.com

Oh Happy Day
www.jordanferney.blogspot.com

Stone Barns Center for Food and Agriculture
www.stonebarnscenter.org

Sunday Suppers
www.sunday-suppers.com

A Way to Garden.com
http://awaytogarden.com

Help with Identifying Invasive Plants

Center for Invasive Species and Ecosystem Health
229-386-3298
www.invasive.org

Nurseries

Avant Gardens
South Dartmouth, Massachusetts
508-998-8819
www.avantgardensne.com

Brent and Becky's Bulbs
Gloucester, Virginia
877-661-2852
www.brentandbeckysbulbs.com

The Flower Company
Kittery, Maine
207-439-4023
www.flowerco.com

Forestfarm
Williams, Oregon
541-846-7269
www.forestfarm.com

Glover Perennials LLC
Cutchogue, New York
613-765-3546
www.gloverperennials.com

Opus Plants
Little Compton, Rhode Island
403-635-2074
www.opustopiarium.com

Quansett Nurseries, Inc.
South Dartmouth, Massachusetts
800-636-6931
www.quansettnurseries.com

Snug Harbor Farm
Kennebunkport, Maine
207-967-2414
http://snugharborfarm.blogspot.com

Van Berkum Nursery
Deerfield, New Hampshire
603-463-7663
www.vanberkumnursery.com

Vessel Resources

Campania International, Inc.
Pennsburg, Pennsylvania
215-541-4627
http://campaniainternational.com

Domani
Lokeren, Belgium
+32-(0)9-340-45-00
www.domani.be

Elegant Earth
Birmingham, Alabama
800-242-7758
www.elegantearth.com

Out-Standing
Malle, Belgium
+32-(0)3-385-57-74
www.out-standing.be

INDEX

Page references in *italics* indicate photographs.

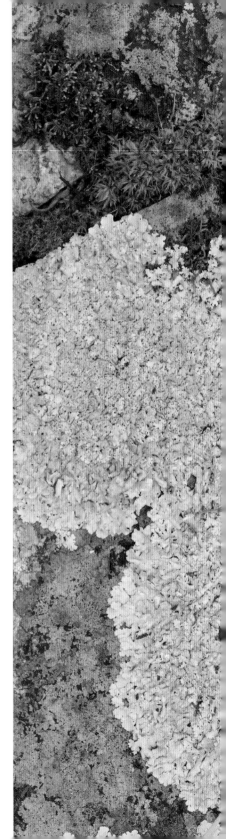

Other Storey Titles You Will Enjoy

Covering Ground, by Barbara W. Ellis.
Creative ideas to landscape with hardworking and attractive ground covers.
224 pages. Paper. ISBN 978-1-58017-665-1.

Designer Plant Combinations, by Scott Calhoun.
More than 100 creative combinations top garden designers that will inspire
home gardeners.
240 pages. Paper. ISBN 978-1-60342-077-8.

Fallscaping, by Nancy J. Ondra and Stephanie Cohen.
A comprehensive guide to the best plants for brightening late-season landscapes.
240 pages. Paper with flaps. ISBN 978-1-58017-680-4.

Foliage, by Nancy J. Ondra.
An eye-opening garden guide to the brilliant colors and textures of dozens of
plants, all chosen for the unique appeal of their leaves.
304 pages. Paper with flaps. ISBN 978-1-58017-648-4.
Hardcover with jacket. ISBN 978-1-58017-654-5.

Tabletop Gardens, by Rosemary McCreary.
Designs for 40 dazzling tabletop gardens to inspire the indoor green thumb
year-round.
168 pages. Paper with flaps. ISBN 978-1-58017-837-2.

Window Boxes Indoors & Out, by James Cramer & Dean Johnson.
Full-color photographs, step-by-step instructions, and quick design ideas for
year-round window boxes.
176 pages. Paper. ISBN 978-1-58017-518-0.

These and other books from Storey Publishing are available
wherever quality books are sold or by calling 1-800-441-5700.
Visit us at *www.storey.com.*